M000222801

"Probably the single most impor[tant thing I learned in] my life was how to get outside of [it,] that Gene had written his book when I was struggling so much. You have the opportunity to Avoid the Success Trap by reading this book. I promise you won't be disappointed."

— **Howard Behar, President Starbucks, Retired**

"A friend once told me that success traps are harder to get out of than failure traps. This is brilliantly illustrated in Gene Hammett's raw and authentic book. Be careful: this might just change your life!"

— **Greg McKeown, New York Times Bestselling Author of** *Essentialism: The Disciplined Pursuit of Less*

"What a fascinating story! Gene Hammett's journey is inspiring to us all. He shares the common enemies that we must overcome to keep growing."

— **Dee Ann Turner, VP of Enterprise Social Responsibility of Chick-fil-A and Bestselling Author of** *It's My Pleasure, The Impact of Extraordinary Talent and a Compelling Culture*

"Gene Hammett works from the depths of his heart, from a place of openness with the facts instead of his hopes, and with a massive body of knowledge gathered from his experiences and the countless interviews he's conducted with leaders. What you get with The Trap of Success is a great tool for getting yourself out of your own traps and back on the path to what matters most."

— **Chris Brogan, New York Times Bestselling Author of** *The Freaks Shall Inherit the Earth*

"For many of us, we've been taught to follow the beaten path because it's supposed to be safe. Gene's candid stories around losing millions and his path back coupled with the experiences and insights from clients as well as guests on his popular podcast, Leaders in the Trenches, teach and inspire you to overcome the fear that keeps you from living a professional life of significance and impact."

— **Jordan Harbinger, Host of *The Art of Charm* Podcast**


"As Gene Hammett shows in this terrific book, we must have the courage to break from what we have always done to create more impact in this world. Stop waiting and start doing."

— **Dr. Jonah Berger, Marketing Professor at the Wharton School at the University of Pennsylvania and Best Selling Author of *Contagious* and *Invisible Influence***

# THE TRAP
## OF
## SUCCESS

A Brutally Candid Guide to Overcoming
Your Fears, Finding Significance, and
Attaining Profound Success

## GENE HAMMETT

© 2017 by Core Elevation, Inc.
http://www.coreelevation.com

Published by Core Elevation, Inc.
2897 N. Druid Hills Rd, #188 Atlanta, GA 30329

Editing by Tim Walker
Interior Design by Derek Hart, Get the Gigs (http://GettheGigs.com)
Cover by VOVO Designs.

ISBN: 978-0-9894888-1-5 (paperback)
ISBN: 978-0-9894888-4-6 (ebook)

For information about special discounts available for bulk purchases, sales promotions, fund-raising and educational needs, contact Core Elevation, Inc. at 1-678-242-9957 or mary@leadersinthetrenches.com.

Visit the author's website at www.genehammett.com.

# DEDICATION

Sharing this book with you would not be possible without those in my life that have supported me and believed in me.

To each one of my clients that gave of yourselves beyond what you believed possible. There are too many to name. Each of you knows who you are and what you mean to me. Each of you played a part in my journey of significance. Allowing me to impact you has had a profound impact on me. Thank you.

The ups and downs of life would not be the same without the love of my parents, Gloria and Wendell. The effect of your love is something that has shaped who I am as a person. My Dad is no longer with us. I will always carry a piece of you in my heart. Mom, you are the most giving person I know, and I want you to know how much I love you. I could not have asked for better parents.

Now for my wife who has been there through the doubt and fear... the good and the bad. You encouraged me to get back up after losing it all with tenderness and sometimes being brutally candid (of course, I needed it). You loved me when I felt unlovable. Amanda, you endured more than most could handle and with this, I say to you with my whole heart...I love you.

To God, you were there when life was dark. You are my light. I strive to follow the path you sent me here to walk.

# TABLE OF CONTENTS

# INTRODUCTION

(This gets a little personal, if you want to skip and jump to the heart of the book you can start at Chapter 1.)

I was waiting for the most important call of my life.

If everything panned out, my company would make just over a million dollars.

Then, the phone rang. It was my business partner: "We have a problem..."

As he began to explain what had happened, the blood drained from my face, and I felt a sharp pain in the pit of my stomach. We had been working on this deal for 18 months, and now everything had blown up in a moment. I collapsed on the edge of my bed and buried my face in my hands. *Was this really happening to me?*

I'm not sure if I blacked out, but I don't remember anything else about that call.

I did know that it was going to change me forever. I now refer to that day as the "2x4 day"—the day I got hit upside the head with a 2x4. I learned the hard way that that's what it feels like when you *lose* $3 million instead of *making* $1 million on the biggest deal of your life.

Losing that much money—well, there's no way it could be *good*. But then it got worse: my wife asked me, "Are we going to be okay?" I've never felt more shame than when I had to admit to the love of my life, "I don't think so." I couldn't help but wonder if she would leave me and take our two-year-old boy with her.

The weeks and months that followed that failed deal were the hardest of my life. The abrupt crisis that ended the deal created legal problems for me, to put it mildly. I lost my business, my savings, my house. But worst of all—I lost my confidence. I lay in bed for days, doing nothing but feeling the gravity of what I caused, not just for myself but for thousands of clients who had given me their money and their trust. For five years after that, every time I stepped out of my house, I worried that someone would run up to me and shoot me in the head. When I went for a jog, I wondered if someone was following behind me. My mind would keep asking, "Is today the day?"

Yet I would never be where I am today without that traumatic experience. When you lose everything, you are forced to change. It took a long time to find peace in that, but now I know:

**The worst thing ever to happen to me became the greatest gift I ever received.**

It set me on the path that has become my life's work: transcending my old, limited view of success to discover the much more important dance between breakthrough success and—most important of all—true significance.

In other words, losing it all gave me a chance to find out what really mattered and create a new life, one in which I am fulfilled and living up to my fullest potential.

But let's look a little more closely at how I got here.

### Setting the Trap for Myself with My First Business

In 2001, I started a service business with just an idea—selling tickets and travel packages to corporate clients for the world's largest sporting events. By the end of my first full year of business, I had logged $1 million in sales, built a team of employees, and traveled all over the world.

For years, I kept at it, increasing my revenues and reaching the point where I could run the business and still have time to pursue outside interests such as Brazilian Jiu Jitsu and Muay Thai boxing. At the 2008 Beijing Olympics, we supplied tickets to more than 8,500 people, netting over $1 million in profits for my partners and myself in one event. Buoyed by that success, I decided to go for the biggest deal of my life at the 2010 Vancouver Olympics.

Over the years, I had developed the contacts, partners, and skills to pull off a deal of that size. I had the industry reputation needed to put together a contract that big. I had worked six Olympics before, so I knew the ins and outs of events at that scale.

So I got to work.

## Losing Everything

On January 15th, 2010, more than a year of work was about to come to fruition. That work had started right after the Beijing Olympics. My partner and I negotiated a contract for Vancouver that documented all the terms of payment and delivery for thousands of tickets. I began offering these tickets for sale to my long-term clients and other ticket resellers in the industry. It was not easy to sell thousands of tickets in the midst of the 2008–2009 financial downturn, but I worked this opportunity like my life depended on it.

I moved my wife, our son, and my whole office to Vancouver in December 2009 to set up for the Games. The demand for tickets continued to increase, and my position with tickets was solid. I had never received so many tickets for an event at one time, so I hired new employees and invested money in office space just to make the deal possible. I never doubted for a second that my partner would come through, just as our contract stated.

In the final days before the Vancouver Games began, I negotiated the sale of a huge block of tickets so that I would have all the money needed to pick up the tickets. I was ready with the final payment.

As I waited for the call from my partner with the final details, I was in Vancouver with all the pieces of the business ready...and that was "2x4 day"—the day everything changed. My partner's story began to unravel, and the untruths began to come out. I became obsessed with every name and detail he had shared with me, and began to realize that what I believed to be true was in fact a huge set-up.

The tickets never showed up, and the nearly $3 million I had paid on the contract was gone.

Worse, it wasn't just my money. I had more than 10,000 clients who depended on me—who had paid for their tickets in advance based on the now-worthless contract I held in my hands.

Technically, the legal term for what happened is "breach of contract," but I think of it as "the squeeze." I was caught between one supplier and thousands of honest people I had made promises to in good faith.

The next few weeks were excruciating. For nearly four hours, I was questioned by the Secret Service—the only law-enforcement agency with international jurisdiction. Finally, they realized that I was a victim, not a perpetrator, of fraud. Then they began their investigation into the missing tickets and the breached contract. My legal team of James Moriarty, Filippo Marchino, and Damon Rogers stepped in to help, beginning a court battle that lasted almost five years. During the whole time that we tried to recover the money of the customers who had trusted me, my attorneys were like knights. They put up a fight when no one else would.

Still, shame and disappointment consumed me with every breath.

## Coming Back from the Brink of Death

The journey back was hard and riddled with uncertainty. In many ways, it did feel like my career and standing as a businessperson had died. I had no idea how I would pay my bills—not just legal fees, but for a place to rest my head, food to eat, and utilities to live.

I did know one thing: I wanted to work for myself again. I would work my *own* way back as an entrepreneur. But I also knew that I wanted a different kind of business, one that was based on truly serving people, not just on transactions and sales.

As I thought of how I would come back, I remembered a quote from the great Maya Angelou:
*"People will forget what you said, people will forget what you did, but people will never forget how you made them feel."*
—**Maya Angelou**, Award-Winning Poet and Presidential Medal of Freedom Recipient

Her words helped me realize the changes I needed to make in my life—professionally and personally. Indeed, I wanted to make certain that my new professional direction aligned fully with who I wanted to be *as* a person.

Before the "2x4 day," I lacked a real purpose. I had success, but it was shallow and without any personal significance. I look back now and realize that, even with all the money I was making, I was not taking action to create the life I wanted.

I was trapped in my success.

One way to see this is to look at what kept me from taking new actions. With the benefit of hindsight, I can look back now and see that I was stuck in my comfort zone. Back then, I didn't have the courage to create a different kind of business. I was constantly stressed and wasn't fulfilled by what I was doing. Even though I hated my business, it always felt like I was making too much money to step away from it.

Then I remembered a time in my career when I had sought out a business coach who had helped me think through the strategies I used to build that multi-million-dollar ticket business. I thought about how rewarding it would be to do the same for someone else—but with the added dimension of helping people find not just surface-level business success, but deeper significance in their work.

## THE TRAP OF SUCCESS

Finally, I realized that I should become a coach. Coaching would be my way to serve and contribute to the world and humanity, and a way for *me* to feel significant. I felt like coaching was aligned with my purpose and would fulfill me in many dimensions.

I was shifting inside, away from being a hardcore deal maker and toward being a more attentive caregiver. That shift set me on the path I'm still on, balancing the two sides of my work—toward success and significance—as needed with my clients.

I invested the last bit of my money to join a training program for coaches. At times, it felt selfish to spend money on education, given that my family and I struggled to pay the bills and we were losing our home. But that training is what I needed on a personal level to overcome my doubts and fears.

### The Need to Forgive

Six months after the breach of contract, I sought forgiveness from everyone involved in the ordeal. My coach training had led me to see beyond the surface level of life. I started to develop a new awareness of the struggle inside me—a struggle that I needed to resolve so I could enter the next stage of my journey. Finding forgiveness was a key part of that.

I wanted to move on and let go of the past. However, the pain was still fresh, and the daily struggle to make ends meet and regain my confidence kept me stuck in thoughts of failure and revenge. I needed to adopt a different outlook, or I would never be free in my mind.

This is where I was able to test the power of coaching against my own need to forgive, heal, and move on. My journey back to confidence could only begin by forgiving myself.

With my new coaching friends and mentors, I talked about letting go of the past to move forward. I watched as my friends dealt with their own challenges and setbacks. That led to the powerful realization that my struggle was not completely unique. Yes, I was the only one who was dealing with a financial loss of that magnitude. But I could see that some of the other issues my friends were navigating were similar to my own.

## Serving Others

I found my way out in *service*. Since 2010, I have had the pleasure of helping leaders transform their thinking and strategies to build businesses beyond what they thought was possible. The founders, leaders, and CEOs I work with already have *some* success in business, but they also know that there is more out there—that breakthrough success and a real sense of significance awaits them. My aim is to help them get there by creating small shifts that lead to the biggest results.

From working one-on-one with clients to interviewing leaders on my podcast, *Leaders in the Trenches*, to sharing my message as a speaker, I am thrilled to be part of so many people's businesses and personal growth. This thrill is such a huge part of who I am now that it has become my purpose in life.

Losing everything is not the path I would recommend for shifting your life to a higher sense of purpose. But that's what it took for me to change at my core. The change has allowed me to help thousands of business owners make more money, hire elite teams, and become more powerful leaders, while deepening their sense that they have real meaning in the world—that their work truly has significance.

The emotional payoff for me has been huge. It has been incredible to witness so much growth in others and to know that I've helped foster it. It's something I can take pride in—a wonderful reward for the resilience and courage required to pursue my own journey over the past seven years.

I hope that you never have to start over like me. Whatever your specific path, you can look forward to a journey of growth and learning that is sure to pay off if you are willing to embrace your own resilience and courage.

# THE TRAP OF SUCCESS

## Why this book?

My reason for writing *The Trap of Success* is simple: I hate to see people struggle in their lives because they are afraid to go after what they want. I've seen how the common approach to success can leave you feeling empty and unfulfilled once you achieve some basic markers of traditional success, for example a certain level of income, or owning a particular make of car, or having a "nice" house in the "right" neighborhood.

If this describes your situation, you are not alone. It is common for high achievers to drift after they have "made it." Thinking about how traditional success can become a trap sparks a new conversation that is played out within this book. Crucially, the book also introduces how significance and success can actually feed each other in your life's work—but only if you commit yourself to escaping the trap.

Given my training, my mindset, and especially the experience of my own painful setbacks, it's easy for me to see what an amazing impact people can have when they show the courage to think differently and take resilient action toward a purpose-filled life—a life of significance. I have watched many individuals make that transformation, and I am heartbroken every time I see someone of talent and ability who won't make the commitment to do it for themselves.

I was one of those people—too afraid to let go of the shallow success I had to create a life of significance. I made tons of money in my international sports tour business, but my sense of security with my income and lifestyle meant that I couldn't bring myself to leave an industry I actually hated.

Starting over at 39 and building a new kind of business pushed me to the edge of my comfort zone and beyond. I want to share my journey with you, which means sharing a lot of joyful moments and breakthroughs that helped me develop a new way of living, and a new way of making a living. But I'll share the painful parts, too, because sometimes pain is the most powerful path to growth.

Throughout this book, I include vignettes from clients I have personally witnessed make similar changes. I have also been lucky enough to interview hundreds of amazing entrepreneurs and visionary leaders for my podcast, so I will include parts of their journeys, too. This will allow you to see a variety of transformational moments that you can relate back to your own life.

I've worked hard to create my new business as a business coach, and to keep pushing my own boundaries. The day-to-day world of entrepreneurship is filled with opportunities to go beyond our comfort zones, and we must take those opportunities whenever they come along.

All transformative success—including innovation, creativity, and personal growth—requires you to expand your boundaries of comfort. The things that scare you or cause you doubt are likely the very things that you *must* pursue to create the business and life you want.

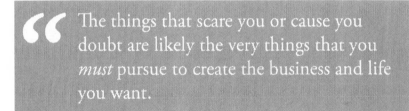

> The things that scare you or cause you doubt are likely the very things that you *must* pursue to create the business and life you want.

This book is about how to break free from your own comfort zone of shallow success so you can find your way to the place where deep success dances with true significance.

# PROLOGUE
# WHAT IF YOU WORK IN A
# BIG CORPORATION?

No one is immune to The Trap of Success. We see it happen
for solopreneurs, owners of small businesses, and leaders within
corporations alike. Heck, even our clubs, teams, and churches can fall
into a drift of complacency.

Looking at corporations, you can see this all the time. Big companies
are so often resistant to change, even when it's clearly necessary. They
deny the importance of innovations until they are impossible to ignore.
Corporations are usually all about hitting the quarterly numbers...and
often forget about the impact they are here to make in the world.

The Trap of Success arises when we rest on the laurels of our previous
accomplishments. When we're in the trap, we press on with the old
way just because it is what worked in the past. We focus on simplistic
success metrics and don't get clearly aligned with our real significance.
That's true regardless of the size of the company we work for, and
regardless of whether we're the one running the show or some other
role. (To put it another way, you're *always* responsible for running your
own show, whether you admit that to yourself or not.)

As you go through this book, look for ways your company can
challenge the status quo. You will find that much of the book is aimed
at a personal level. That's done on purpose. I believe that real change
starts with one person who has the courage to inspire others to a new
future, even when others don't see it yet. That is what leadership is.
Remember that real leadership does not require a title. It requires the
courage to do something never done before and engage others to help
you build it.

## THE TRAP OF SUCCESS

Look for ways you can bring this message to your company that will allow you to clearly define the significance the company can have in the world. There are two huge payoffs for this:

1. Finding the kind of significance that engages teams, departments, operating units, and the corporation as a whole will align people to something bigger than the numbers of traditional success.
2. When you discover the right rhythm of thoughts you have and actions you take, the success of the business will *dance* with its significance. The two of them will feed off of each other, creating exponential success in traditional terms, but also a much deeper impact on the world.

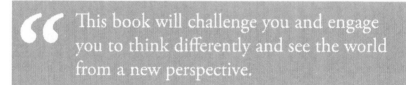

> This book will challenge you and engage you to think differently and see the world from a new perspective.

You picked up this book for a reason. You have likely already heard a calling to do something or create something that fulfills you, but maybe you have ignored it so far. There is something that you want to learn and do and *be* that will have a lasting impact in the world. This book will challenge you and engage you to think differently and see the world from a new perspective. It will ask you to stop drifting along with the current and create a new world where you and those around you are impacted through your work. And you don't get off the hook for that just because you work inside a big corporation.

This book is not just for entrepreneurs, because big companies get trapped by success, too. It is up to you to unlock the potential of your organization.

Are you ready to take that responsibility?

# 1

# THE PURSUIT OF SIGNIFICANCE

Take risks now and do something bold. You won't regret it.

**-Elon Musk, Entrepreneurial Pioneer and Business Magnate**

## THE TRAP OF SUCCESS

Before we can even talk about success—we have to talk about the real goal, the bigger goal, for your work, your career, and your life: **significance.**

If I've discovered anything through my own setbacks in life, it's that aiming for anything less than significance guarantees that you'll fall short of the fulfillment and satisfaction you crave and deserve. And that's true no matter how "successful" you become. So we may as well start by getting clear on the bigger picture of what we're pursuing.

Waking up every day to live a life of significance might be more like a dream for you. I understand that completely, because it certainly didn't seem possible for me for many years of my career.

Simply gunning for success takes up so much of your time and energy. There is so much to do. There are so many opportunities: people to meet, deals to close, money to make. Hundreds of emails to plow through every day. You're pulled in all directions. But most of these things, if you're really honest with yourself, are distracting you from what is most important.

There can be a different way. In fact, there *needs* to be a different way.

Imagine getting out of bed every morning filled with a sense of purpose, knowing that your work is making an impact. You have an abundant sense that you matter. You are living your calling.

You are stepping up to your potential—your *real* potential.

Think of the impacts on your work. When you make decisions throughout the day, you no longer make them only because of the money you will earn or the fame that you hope will shine down on you. You make decisions based on the *difference* they will make, and the people you are here to serve.

Significance makes every Monday a joy as you get to start anew by using your talents for the betterment of humankind.

Extend this feeling into the future, to a time when your significance resonates with your material success, allowing you to be generous with no concern for what comes back in return. You give to charities, you give to people, and you give to yourself.

You have the freedom to do the work that inspires you, leaving the other stuff for someone else.

You are living your life the way it was meant to be lived. You are living your mission.

How does that version of life feel for you?

### I Wanted More

If you'd asked me that question ten years ago, I would have said that it felt great to imagine it...but that it was really just a pipe dream. No matter how much I may have wanted to achieve significance as a successful entrepreneur, I could never let it happen when I was running my first business.

I had success. I had financial freedom and time freedom. I had as much money as I needed to live with comfort, and I created a lifestyle for myself and my family that I was happy enough with. Yet I also created barriers inside my head that stopped me from going for what I really wanted.

 Significance is a feeling from within. You know when you have it, and can feel its absence when you don't.

Doing the right thing is not always the most profitable. Doing the right thing is rarely easy. But doing the right thing—even when it isn't lucrative, even when it's hard—is what puts you on the path to significance.

## THE TRAP OF SUCCESS

"Significance" is a tough word to get our heads around because it's not easily defined or measured. Significance is a feeling from within. You know when you have it, and can feel its absence when you don't. Here's the full definition of "significance" from the Merriam-Webster Dictionary:

1.  a : something that is conveyed as a meaning often obscurely or indirectly
    b : the quality of conveying or implying
2.  a : the quality of being important : moment
    b : the quality of being statistically significant

To think of it from another angle, Tony Robbins describes significance as "feeling unique, important, special, or needed." I would add that significance goes along with the need to contribute to others.

I would also point out that significance ebbs and flows with you, depending on your focus. When you focus on life's frustrations or struggles, you feel common, unimportant, and irrelevant. When you decide to focus on the value you create and the impact you make, you feel significant.

There was a reason that I couldn't get out of bed on some of the darkest days after my first business collapsed. I was so focused on the bad in my life that I couldn't see even the possibility of the good. That is how focus works.

But what if I told you that you have a choice about where to put your focus? You can focus on the struggle you face...or on the impact you could have.

Which would you choose?

Let's look at other aspects of significance.

### Freedom

Significance includes a sense of freedom. It is hard to feel the power of significance if you feel trapped by your to-do list or by the choices you've already made.

Freedom is the primary reason that people start businesses. Having the freedom to do the work you *want* to do instead of the work you *have* to do is huge. But even an entrepreneurial business can become a trap if it doesn't align with your bigger ideas about making a difference in the world. When your days are filled with work that doesn't inspire you or give you energy, you will struggle to find significance.

### Innovation

Creating something new and unique is also part of significance. Doing the same thing as everyone else, even with incremental improvement, is not innovation. I emphasize "new and unique" because innovation requires boldness in approaching old problems—doing what has never been done.

Significance and innovation go hand in hand as you push into new areas. People like Steve Jobs and Elon Musk learned that their contribution to the world comes from driving innovation.

To be an innovator, you don't have to change the way we make phone calls. Nor do you have to create a new form of transportation or build a rocket to Mars. But in the business world, you do need to push the boundaries beyond what is traditional or commonplace if you want to feel significant.

### Money

Money often adds to significance, but it is not required.

You can have money and not feel significant; conversely, you can feel significant without an abundance of money. I've felt significant with very little in my bank account, and I've felt insignificant while closing million-dollar deals.

## THE TRAP OF SUCCESS

If all you care about is money, this may be hard to understand. Don't get me wrong: money is a part of our lives, and an important part. You can't pay your mortgage with hugs, nor can you save for a rainy day with smiles. If you are struggling with the basics of life like food, shelter, and security, it is hard to be focused on the bigger goals. That's compounded when you are providing for others in your family.

However, true significance is about so much more than money. It is a sense of worthiness, a deep and grounded understanding that you are making a difference in the world.

### The Journey of Significance

The journey is not the same for everyone. We all have different paths and start at different points. We will encounter different challenges as well.

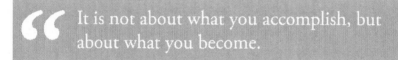

> " It is not about what you accomplish, but about what you become.

This means that there is no end to the path. You keep going and discovering new challenges. You continue to grow, and you evolve as a person. It is not about what you accomplish, but about what you become. It is less about what others see in you and more about how you feel about yourself. On the journey of significance, it is about being fulfilled with who you are.

But I am sure that it is a journey, because the feeling of significance is gone in a flash if you are not careful and intentional about it.

How do we know it is not about a destination? Because it's so easy to "arrive" at the destination you had defined as important, only to find out that owning your own business, earning a million dollars a year, winning the big award, completing the advanced degree, or whatever else you had aimed for...doesn't bring you a feeling of significance.

The journey of significance can take many forms.

For some, it could be creating or building a non-profit. One example of this is Tony Robbins' mission to feed 42 million people over the past seven years. Tony has used that mission as a driving force in his life and his business.

For others, it could be the impact you have in your immediate community and personal circles. Being significant to your family is a given for most people. I get it—I love my family. And family is likely important to you; however, it is not the only reason you are here.

For the startups, the journey is about creating businesses that innovate for the way we live and interact with each other. There are thousands of new technologies that we use for this every day—tools that didn't even exist a few years ago. You don't have to be Mark Zuckerberg of Facebook for this to apply to you. You can innovate in your own market or niche. If you are a founder, surely you see what you do as significant to the world.

If you are like me, the journey of significance comes through working with others in a transformative way. I am overjoyed by helping leaders and teams see new strategies and remove the foggy thinking that keeps them stuck.

It can take a while to understand exactly where your own feeling of significance lies, as I have learned from experience. In the process of writing this book, I read through dozens of old journals and looked over backups of old hard drives. I discovered something that I wrote in early 2009 (just before my "2x4 day") that I wanted to share with you. It was from a coach I worked with back then. He asked me a series of questions before we started working together. One of them was:

*What dream or goal have you given up on?*

When I looked at the list I made back then of dreams I was no longer pursuing, I noticed that at the top was "Be a coach." That's interesting, because at the time I was making tons of money and had the freedom in my life to do what I wanted. But I was so set in my ways that I gave up on a dream that had real meaning and purpose attached to it. I share this with you because we all have dreams that we give up on...and often we give up for the wrong reasons.

Ten years ago, I didn't know it was possible for me to be a coach, but now I can't imagine *not* doing it for the rest of my life.

You have likely given up something that was a dream of yours, or otherwise really important to you, to be the person that you are now.

It is easy to let other things get in the way, especially when money is involved. But finding significance is a journey that goes far beyond making a living. In fact, I am going to show you how significance is essential to making a life *and* making a living at the same time.

During that journey, you must face many internal and external battles. Here is one way to look at the battles that go on inside you.

### Your Inner Critic

The internal battle usually comes from that little voice inside you that wants you to doubt yourself and fear change. I call that voice the "**inner critic.**"

That inner critic exists inside of each us, and it is annoying and persistent. I say this with a smile, but we all know your inner critic is an asshole.

Sure, "asshole" is a strong word. Yet after interacting with thousands of people, and realizing that this destructive inner voice is what gets in the way of people achieving their goals, I'm comfortable with using it, because your inner critic does not play nice—it plays dirty.

## Significance Flows In and Out

Significance is not something that I feel all the time, even though I feel it more now than I ever did before.

In my previous business, I was living in the trap of success, always wanting significance but feeling like I could never have it. I felt successful—confident, even. But I didn't feel like I was making a difference in the world.

That's one big reason for writing this book. In the work I do today, I love coaching and speaking to people to inspire them to see new perspectives and challenge their old ways of thinking, because I love being a part of others' growth. I can see the transformation so clearly that sometimes I tear up when my clients share their breakthroughs with me. The reaction is even stronger when I talk to them years later and they have continued to evolve and achieve new milestones.

Yet significance is still a journey, and I still endure the day-to-day trials it takes to create any business—much less a transformational business. The last seven years of building my coaching and speaking business have tested me. When I got started, I felt uncertainty and doubt for many months, wondering how I would pay the bills. I remember the times when I was doing about $3,000 per month in sales and had about $1,500 per month in expenses.

It is nearly impossible for a family of three to live in Atlanta on $1,500 in take-home pay each month. At the same time, my clients were adding $10,000 per month to their revenue with ease. Some were doubling and tripling the income of their businesses. Think about that for a moment: I was struggling to pay my bills, while my clients were thrilled with their results. I felt significant in my work, but nearly worthless in my promise to provide for my family—not very successful.

The ups and downs of any business are part of the process, of course. I deeply love what I do, which is what makes it possible to face the continual tests of courage and resilience.

21

## THE TRAP OF SUCCESS

Yet my work still has to provide for my family, and that means money is an important part of the equation. There has to be *enough* money. And the truth is that significance is not always the most profitable decision, even as we grow. But the reward for significance is greater than what extra money in the bank can give you.

### Confessions of a People Pleaser

For as much as significance is about impacting others, it is also about self-worthiness.

> Significance is about finding the harmony between your own vision of life and the need to live in a world that you are changing.

Wanting to feel worthy is something that tends to grab us and point us in the direction of being liked. Yet significance is not just about being liked, because the need to be liked puts the focus on your own ego. Significance is about finding the harmony between your own vision of life and the need to live in a world that you are changing. Finding that harmony calls for a sense of worth that comes from deep inside, not one that's always dependent on others' judgments of you.

Yet I am a people pleaser, through and through. I want to be liked. I get this from growing up being taught to be "nice" and wanting to fit in.

In high school, even though I had many friends and good grades, I was a bit of a nerd. I remember, during my junior year, when the decision to go to prom came around. I had someone in mind to ask, but never found the courage to do it, so I let the moment pass.

I never went to prom that year. I worked instead. This was my pattern—I would take the money instead of taking the emotional risk. Thinking back, I realize that I feared what others would think of me. It was more comfortable to risk nothing than to risk rejection.

That pattern repeated itself for senior prom. I let the fear of rejection keep me from making a move. I didn't want anyone else to see my pain and make fun of me, so I never told anyone how I felt. I skipped that prom, too. As I remember, I choose to work that night so I could pocket the money.

In the bigger picture, I didn't feel worthy during those years of my life.

Maybe you went to your prom, and maybe you didn't grow up being a nerd. However, you surely faced your own moments when you played it safe and chose to live in comfort rather than taking the risk. This is natural on the journey of life.

Today, I am a different person—very different. Because of what I've been through, and because I'm now so focused on balancing significance with success, I've broken through those fears and put myself on the line again and again. Now I use big stages to share my message, without concern for being liked. I coach people, and sometimes I am the one who shines a light into the dark corners they'd rather not explore. To be honest, most people are uncomfortable examining the dark elements of their life. At times, it causes them to be annoyed at me. But they often appreciate it later.

I know that not everyone in my world is happy with me, and that's okay. I have learned to detach from their actions and behaviors. It's tied to a deeper lesson I've learned, which is that, when you show up as a leader, you can only help others see new perspectives; you can't make them do anything about it. As a coach, my job is only to help my clients see new choices with clarity—not to force them to take action, much less try to get them to always like me. I have to let them take full ownership for their success or failure. Worrying about what they're thinking of me in those coaching moments would be harmful to our work.

It is impossible to be liked by everyone when you want to be helpful. This book embodies that. It's a deep reflection of who I am and of my life's journey. I'm giving this to you because I want you to know that you can find significance—and that you are not alone in seeking it, or in struggling to find it.

Significance is about the internal feeling that you and your work matter—that's what I mean by self-worthiness. In a crazy-busy world, feeling significant has to be done with intention. That means you have to purposely choose to grow as a person. You have to choose to push beyond the boundaries of comfort and strive to make an impact in this world.

Indulge me while I take you deeper into my life, back to the beginning of my professional career, to explain how I came to these realizations.

### Starting Out in Corporate America

My story is probably not unlike yours. I began my career working to fulfill other people's goals and dreams. (I love that description of what it means to have a job.) I'm keenly aware that getting a paycheck is a huge priority for many people, and that it's often the right thing to do. Some people are meant to work for others, and you can definitely still find significance while you do that. (See the Prologue for more.)

My nine years in corporate America definitely had a purpose, because I gained the skills that would serve me as a business owner. I took it upon myself to align my professional goals with the goals of the companies I worked for, and I didn't see work as just a nine-to-five job. I was there to learn and grow by taking on new responsibilities. This made me a great employee, and I landed numerous promotions and new opportunities.

The important thing is that I did it for me, not the companies I was working for. I was engaged in my work to prepare for my real love: being an entrepreneur.

I started out in strategic consulting. In my work as a consultant, I wanted to gain as much experience as possible, as fast as possible. I tackled a variety of projects. I worked on mergers and acquisitions that were worth hundreds of millions of dollars. I carried out deep research, writing two books with my colleagues. I even wrote one book essentially on my own at the age of 24. I consulted on dozens of projects and interacted at the highest levels within companies. I took on responsibilities that allowed me to grow and prepared me to be an entrepreneur.

With the emergence of the Internet, I developed a thirst to understand technology. I worked for a Web design and development company in 1996. The company made websites; my job was to sell them. I was on the bleeding edge of this new movement, but it's a challenge when you make a living selling something to people who don't know what it is (and who certainly didn't understand its value, back then).

I changed jobs to get a more complete understanding of technology and worked for what would become PricewaterhouseCoopers in their emerging technology sector. Again, the work gave me experience that I would later use to launch my company.

The last stop on my journey through corporate America came when I worked with a dotcom company, NetVendor, in the boom era of 1999 to 2001. We raised a few rounds of venture capital, and as employee number 27, I had a key role in sales that brought the first waves of e-commerce to Fortune 1000 brands. You've probably never heard of NetVendor, because we didn't "make it" in the traditional sense. Certainly, it would have made my transition into entrepreneurship far easier if I had been at Google, Amazon, or some other well-known company with a massive IPO.

Regardless, it was a fun ride. The excitement of working with the Internet and large brands to make their products available online in the early days was thrilling. It was the future, and I was right there on the front lines.

In 2001, after the fall of the Twin Towers, business got hard. My company's leadership knew they needed to weather the storm, so they made massive layoffs. Since I was considered a "key employee," I had a contract with a golden parachute. Lucky for me, the company didn't need me anymore. When I was laid off, they handed me a check for about $35,000.

I didn't even consider getting another job. I was ready to go out on my own. I was beyond ready. Now was the time to follow the dream that I had hidden inside myself.

### Early Significance

As I have reflected on my tenure in corporate America, I've thought of where I felt significant. There were certainly times that felt more significant than others. For instance, when I traveled around the country researching and writing, I felt significant to the company and myself. My work was a big part of that year's revenue supporting the other employees at the company.

When I was with the dotcom, I felt significant in my role in sales. I was an integral player in millions of dollars' worth of sales, and I trained a diverse team to support that effort.

Those times were great, as I felt like my work mattered beyond myself. I know that, in the grand scheme of the world, I wasn't righting wrongs like a cop or curing cancer like a doctor. But I felt like my work made a difference. I had pride in what I was doing, and I felt valued.

That's what significance feels like. You don't have to make some grand gesture to have that feeling inside you. You don't have to be Mother Teresa, either. You just have to make a difference that you can be proud of.

### Why Significance?

My professional journey was likely different than yours, though you can likely find some similarities. But whatever path you took, it's important to think about significance right up front because it's absolutely vital for escaping the trap of success. I start this book talking about significance because it can become harder and harder to keep significance firmly in mind as we talk about attaining transformative levels of success in the next stages of the book.

All of that became very clear to me when I lost it all back in 2010. Having lost my success, I realized that what I longed for most was the feeling that I mattered in the world. I wanted to do something that made a difference.

As you'll see in the chapters that follow, before that period of crisis, I spent nine years building a business that was successful when measured in traditional terms. I made good money, and I was happy with the lifestyle I created. I loved that I could train in Brazilian Jiu-Jitsu 15+ hours per week and run my business, too. I provided for my family and made regular contributions to my retirement. I even had a convertible Mercedes. (Boy, do I miss that car.) Many people, looking in from the outside, would have said that I had achieved significance.

But, to be honest with you, I didn't feel it. For all the money and the trappings of success, I didn't feel that my work mattered, or that I was creating something amazing and innovative.

I came to realize that the money I had made was a trap that kept me from reaching significance.

## Your Challenge

When you decide to create a life of significance, you will be challenged in many ways. You have to be willing to take risks that make significance a regular part of your life.

This book emerged from the trap of success that I created for myself in my former business. That trap is likely something you have experienced as well. I have talked to thousands of people about the trap, and I've seen it affect many clients who operate their business from a place of comfort.

## THE TRAP OF SUCCESS

But now it's time to embrace the challenge, to break free from your own trap of success and achieve a deep sense of satisfaction in your work and your life.

As you do that—and as I'll show you—attaining that deeper sense of satisfaction will also open you up to achieving more success than you've previously been able to imagine. That's the thing about pursuing transformative change: it changes everything you are and everything you do. Once you embrace the challenge to pursue significance and escape the trap of success, you'll find that significance and success will "dance" with each other throughout your life and work. It's as though you'll hear new music and find a new rhythm that allows you to attain more and achieve new, profound levels of satisfaction in your career.

### The Dance of Success and Significance

Let me explain this "dance" between significance and success. It is quite common to see success as a stop along the journey to significance. The thinking is "I'll create this success, then I will create significance." For instance, maybe you'll set up your charity after you build your business to a certain size. In general, people tell themselves, "I will do work that matters after _____." (I'll wait while you fill in the blank.)

In other words, significance comes after you have the success of making money and achieving your other goals. By this logic, success is the gate that you must pass through to get to the land of significance.

I lived with this mindset while I ran my business in sports tours. But even when I achieved success, I felt empty inside. I felt like I could do so much more, but the money and time freedom I had kept me stuck in my old habits. I would fight the urge to innovate and do something purposeful with my life out of fear of giving up what I had worked so hard to create.

This is similar to all the people in corporate jobs who get comfortable with the lifestyle and the perceived lack of risk...so they do nothing to stretch themselves and grow. They just keep working on their projects and making their standard raises. I have talked with hundreds of people who relate to the trap of success because they have spent years pushing down the desire to create something amazing in favor of getting that consistent paycheck. You can do both if you want.

I have been looking into the lives of my clients over the last seven years to see how that model of success just has not been working for them. Either they are so determined to get the money that they forget the really important things in life, or they get to a level of success they want and then find that they are comfortable and only want more "success" trophies.

Take a moment to consider this: the idea that you must first achieve success so you can then create significance is a myth. That myth is the wrong way to think about success and significance. Getting success first and then working on significance is the wrong sequence.

Here's a crazy thought...what if there is not a "sequence" that you must follow? It's not 1, 2, 3.

Success and significance go together in creating a life and a business you love. The energy that comes from doing work of significance actually feeds into your success. Success and significance are like two dance partners. The two of them constantly draw energy and rhythm from each other to create something more beautiful and compelling than either could alone.

Besides its ability to impart meaning to your life and work, the power of significance is that it can make you more successful. Within this book, we will explore how you can make success and significance dance together in your work and life.

Ready?

## THE TRAP OF SUCCESS

### Questions to Inspire You

1. Over your professional career, where did you feel the most significant?
2. In which areas of your life is it most important for you to feel significant now?
3. What gets in the way of your feeling of significance? What doubts? What fears?
4. What dream have you given up on?

# THE DEFINITION OF SUCCESS

Success breeds
complacency.
Complacency breeds
failure.

-Andy Stanley, Senior Pastor and Master
Communicator

## THE TRAP OF SUCCESS

This is *not* a book about building a wildly successful business, in the traditional sense.

And it certainly is *not* about how I made millions, and how you can do it too.

This book is about the failure to see the traps we set for ourselves. About how we fail to seek significance, and in so doing cheat ourselves out of deeper fulfillment *and* greater levels of success.

The mechanics of success are unique for each of you—your path is different from my path. So this book gives you a framework to shift how you think about success and significance. You can apply this framework to your own situation, wherever you are.

I wish I had understood the framework when I started my first business more than 15 years ago. Though I reached a high level of conventional success with that business, I was still not happy. In fact, I was obsessed with doing something bigger and more innovative. I wanted to create a game-changer for my industry—to create something that would matter to the world.

I wanted my work to be more than just filling my bank account. I wanted purpose, fulfillment, and significance.

All of that sounds great, right? But the truth is, I wasn't willing to let go of what I had created so I could reach for something greater. Getting stuck in doing what I had always done caused me to lose it all. I had to lose millions to learn this lesson. You may never have lost everything, but you've likely had to start over or make a huge pivot at some point in life that caused you doubt and fear.

Why did I have to lose it all to figure this out? Why does it sometimes take a hard blow to the psyche to get us to wake up to our situations? It's because we have a tendency to *drift* in life. Drift occurs when we get so focused on the day-to-day that we don't see the bigger picture.

Sometimes it takes a shock to the system to bring that bigger picture into focus. But you can take yourself there, without that kind of trauma, by applying the principles of this book.

This book will help you understand your current patterns of thought and behavior so you can break free from your comfort zone, where you tend to be seduced into a series of supposedly safe decisions. Decisions like that keep us from growing, which is bad because growth is an essential part of attaining significance and fulfillment.

## Starting My Own Business

Let me tell you a little more about how I got seduced into the Trap of Success in my first entrepreneurial venture.

My idea, back when I started that first business in 2001, wasn't revolutionary. It was a safe bet, because I set up the business to operate just like my competitors.

As I explained in the Introduction, my business was in tickets and ticket packages, commonly referred to as international sports tours. I sold them to help individuals and large groups attend the world's largest sporting contests: Super Bowls, the Olympics, the World Cup, and other marquee events.

Even if it wasn't very innovative, I knew what I was doing and I executed pretty well. The business grew to more than $1 million in revenue the very first year. I worked hard, took reasonable chances, and invested in my business. I was good at what I did because I knew how to see opportunities that others didn't.

After achieving that traditional degree of success in business, I began to think about what was next—a new set of goals. It wasn't about making more money (I already had plenty) or having more free time (ditto). I wanted to change the way people bought and made decisions about tickets, and change the industry as a whole.

## THE TRAP OF SUCCESS

I talked about it constantly. "There has to be a better way" was all I could think about. It consumed me.

Those seven words became a theme for me starting in 2005. I remember the year distinctly because I steered hard in that direction right after my father passed away. His death hit me at my emotional core. Maybe you've undergone that kind of introspection yourself after a life-changing experience. Moments like that tend to get us to reflect on what are we doing on this Earth. I loved my Dad very much, and losing him to cancer made me want to do something beyond just making money.

I wanted a better way to make a living that was more fulfilling, something that had a purpose and made an impact in the world. I was already thinking about significance, even though I was still a long way from the breakthrough I needed to get there.

The other side of "There has to be a better way" was my desire to innovate. By 2006, the Internet was ubiquitous in our lives. We researched *everything* online, Googling to research anything we cared about, and especially anything we wanted to buy. I wanted to transcend the old way of buying and selling event tickets—to revolutionize the process.

My desire for purpose and my drive for innovation became two opposing forces in my search for "a better way." Underlying this tension was the reality that I had grown to hate the ticket industry. I hated the travel and the risk, but mostly I hated the fact that selling tickets had become solely about making money—in direct conflict with my deeper desire to do something that wasn't just about having a bigger bank account.

I let this conflict play in my thoughts for years. It became a self-sustaining narrative, a fully-detailed "story" of disgust for my work and the whole ticket industry. As that story ran through my head, my obsession with it kept me from moving forward. It was not real, it was not the truth—but I bought into it.

The problem was, I was so absorbed in the industry that I couldn't separate myself from it. In hindsight, I see that creating a better way to make a living and creating a better way to buy and sell tickets were obviously not the same thing. But failing to distinguish between them was part of the problem—one that I couldn't see at the time.

I suffered through that period of life for more than five years. I thought about it. I talked about it to friends and people in the industry. I made plans to change it. **Yet I didn't do anything about it.**

My wife, Amanda, was sick of hearing it, and I don't blame her. I was like a broken record. She asked me one day, "When are you going to do something about it?" That was hard for me to take. I had built a multi-million-dollar business for myself in the ticket industry by taking action. Yet there I was, doing nothing.

Amanda's words made me reflect. I realized that my unresolved internal conversation about this new direction was keeping me from moving forward.

### Trapped in My Success

It came down to one thing: I was trapped in my success. I was making great money and had built a world around me where I had freedom in my business and personal life. I was comfortable where I was—too comfortable.

To be clear, I had kept pushing my business to new levels of profits. I was taking calculated risks by investing more and more into deals. I led my team diligently and built strong relationships with strategic partners. It paid off as I grew the footprint of the business and made more money.

For example, I began working on packages for the 2008 Beijing Olympics about one year before the games started. I had huge contracts for delivery of tickets, including the biggest contract I had ever written. I worked crazy-hard on it and took risks by trusting in others. That was my normal pattern for running the business.

## THE TRAP OF SUCCESS

Ultimately, my company helped more than 8,500 people attend the Olympics in Beijing. I made more than a million dollars during the eight weeks before and during the Games. The two months I lived in Beijing were the hardest I ever worked, but I've never been afraid of hard work.

Looking back, I realize that, for all the extraordinary effort I put in, I was only doing what I knew to be safe. So even though I kept pushing my business to new levels, I was still lodged firmly in my comfort zone.

Fear kept me from moving forward with my grand plans to revolutionize the ticket industry. The inner critic stopped me. I didn't want to lose what I had created, and I was paralyzed at the thought of doing something bigger that didn't work out.

Being trapped by success is like being inside an invisible box. You can't see the walls, but you are still constrained. It seems like you're doing the right things and making the right decisions, but you're always working within tightly circumscribed limits.

I want to make a note here about resilience. There is so much talk about it these days, and resilience is definitely part of the recipe for continued growth. Yet I've noticed something about resilience: we often cope with life by doing more of what is not working, then call it grit or resilience. But toughing it out on principle when you're doing the wrong things does not serve you. It doesn't get you different results.

Looking back, I realize that I lacked **courage**, not resilience. I needed to muster the kind of courage it takes to break free of what I'd always done. I made incremental gains by playing it safe with what I knew, but I didn't have the courage to leap forward exponentially into the unknown.

Here is the painful part of this story: I was afraid to lose it all, so I didn't go for what I wanted...**yet I still lost it all.** Sure, I lost it because I trusted someone who did me wrong, but the point remains: all my focus on playing it safe didn't actually make me safer. I lost $3 million dollars in 24 hours doing what I had always done, and was forced to start over again.

I couldn't see it at that time, but my continued success kept me stagnant in my thinking, so I didn't make the changes or take the chances I knew I should. I was stuck, in both business and life.

### Looking for More

When I realized that the "success" that I was working for was no longer making me happy, I looked inside to figure out what was going on. I wondered, "Is this it?"

Think back: have you ever had a huge goal that you wanted, and then, once you got it...it didn't feel like you thought it would? You may have experienced initial satisfaction, only to find that it quickly faded away.

In my ticket business, I felt that way all the time. I felt empty in my gut and confused in my head. Focusing on money and getting more of it didn't make me feel better about myself, which made me feel even more empty and confused.

Now that I've interviewed hundreds of business leaders for my *Leaders in the Trenches* podcast over the years, I know I'm not alone. I have attended conferences with speakers courageous enough to share similar stories. Many have had those same moments of frustration, and that same overall feeling of being unfulfilled despite the success they had achieved. So often, you'll hear them ask the same question I did, "Once I had success, I wondered, 'Is this it?'"

You're successful, and that in itself is the problem. I know that sounds counterintuitive, but the same things that help you attain something *good* hold you back from what's *extraordinary*. Keep reading to discover the subtle differences between traditional success and exponential success.

## THE TRAP OF SUCCESS

The main point: You can't create a new invention or innovation—in your profession or in your own life—by doing and thinking as you have always done. Extraordinary comes *only* when you challenge the old patterns of thinking.

Before we push beyond the old, limited quest for success, let's dig deeper to see why a narrow definition of success so often becomes the focal point for those striving for more.

### Definition of Success

Let's turn back to the dictionary one more time. Merriam-Webster gives one definition of success as "the fact of getting or achieving wealth, respect, or fame," but that doesn't feel complete.

Money, respect, or fame definitely can be an element of success, but if you think only in those terms, you're limiting yourself.

Here is my attempt to analyze various definitions of success to come up with the most common ways we think about the concept.

**Success is:**
1. the accomplishment of an aim or purpose
2. the attainment of popularity or profit
3. a person or thing that achieves a desired aim or prosperity
4. the outcome of an undertaking

What if we broaden this definition of success to include the idea of significance? The commonly held view of success that we've accepted lacks the element of having an impact on others, and lacks the sense of purpose—of significance—that affecting others creates within us. Success without significance seems too self-centered, which is why the achievement of traditional success can feel so empty.

### Success Is Relative

Keep in mind, too, that your own definition of success will change over time based on your progress in life and your priorities. Success is relative to where you are right now, and thus different for each of us. You want something different than I do, and I want something different than you do. Plus, each of us wants something different than we did ten years ago.

Think about it: If your net worth were all of a sudden $10 million today, you would likely be thrilled. You would call today a success. However, if Bill Gates or Oprah woke up today with a net worth of $10 million, they would be feeling shock and dismay, not satisfaction.

## Success Is About Momentum

One way of understanding success is seeing it as the momentum of life. Momentum is about growth. It is about a change or shift from where you were, whether that is in terms of money or influence. When you have momentum in your professional life, you are better than you were in the past.

It takes a huge amount of courage to create a new future and build this momentum, especially if where you are has become comfortable. When you keep stretching the boundaries of your courage, you expand your comfort zone.

If you stay at it, over time that courage can evolve into bravery. We often use "courage" and "bravery" as synonyms, but in fact the two words are not interchangeable. Courage means moving forward despite the fear you feel; bravery is a state of being fearless.

As you grow, what scared you before will become easy to overcome. With courage and patience, it turns into that fearless attitude—true bravery.

## Incremental and Exponential Success

Gaining success is a goal for nearly every person on the face of the earth. Certainly, those without some sense of direction or goals are not allowed in my life. I say that only semi-jokingly, because I do purposefully surround myself with people who are growing and striving in all areas of life and business.

## THE TRAP OF SUCCESS

We are here to grow. That growth might be in your business, your professional life, your relationships, or your outside interests. Whatever the case, you must think about stretching yourself.

What most people think of as success is actually incremental growth. There is nothing wrong with the incremental. It is comfortable and evolves over time. But we are not looking to stay in the comfort zone. You don't find significance there.

While incremental growth is linear, exponential growth is explosive. Exponential growth is the "hockey stick" that startups aim to achieve—the graph of growth that is flat in the beginning, then rockets up as users, revenue, or profits rise at a rapid pace. That's what investors look for in ideal companies when they are considering writing big checks.

Exponential growth applies to startups and investors, but it also applies to people who aren't raising capital. This is a concept I've explored with Rich Litvin. I had a great interview with Rich on my podcast, then continued the conversation when we later met up in Los Angeles. Rich is a transformational coach to Olympic athletes, presidential candidates, Hollywood film directors, special forces operatives, and serial entrepreneurs.

Rich has delved into "the trap of success" with his clients. He finds that it is common for people to reach a point of conventional success and never make the transition to exponential success. They accept a fixed view of success, and themselves, that keeps them from changing on the inside. Think about that last sentence: "changing from the inside"—by changing your thinking—is the key.

Exponential growth happens when new thinking takes place. Conventional success, which conforms to and reinforces your comfort zone, tends to block that thinking. Rich believes—and I agree—that conventional success is exactly what holds people back from exponential success.

We are meant to expand and grow. That's what life is supposed to be. And it's why you're reading this book.

I have seen the advantages that come from continuously challenging my current status quo—of expanding beyond my comfort zone. I have also seen hundreds of people do the same in my coaching work, and I am still amazed that more people don't lean into this way of being.

So let's unpack different ways that success can trap you.

## Four Different Traps of Success

1) **Incremental Growth** — Being successful gives you confidence to "stay the course" and keep doing what you have been doing. This is the inertia inherent in the status quo, which ironically is the problem: if you stay on the same course, you'll only keep growing by tiny steps, without making breakthroughs. To grow more meaningfully, transformatively, you have to seek out new ways of being and doing to solve the bigger challenges in life—not just roll along on the same track you've been on.

The trap here is not easy to see, because it will feel like you are on the right path.

2) **Limited Vision** — Your vision of a new future comes with a governor. Not the political kind, but the mechanical part installed on an engine to keep it from running too hot and breaking down. Your future is only as big as what you, and your governor, believe is possible. The problem is that most people think too little of themselves to think big.

This trap keeps you playing small and avoiding risk.

3) **Independence** — Getting to where you are now has worked. You may not have done it all on your own, but now you live in a space where you don't need help from others to keep going. That keeps you from seeking out new perspectives, thus inhibiting you from exponential growth.

41

## THE TRAP OF SUCCESS

This trap slows you down, because it becomes all about what *you* can already do.

4) **A Limited Version of Truth** — This trap is about the stories you live in. It is about the way you see the world today. You hold *your* story as *the* truth, and you have not thought about how you made up that story based on your own experiences and your limited view of the world. This is something we all face. There is a difference between *your* truth and the *absolute* truth.

This problem is only made worse when you surround yourself with people who agree with you. Organizations filled with proverbial "yes-men" and "yes-women" struggle to grow consistently, precisely because they are not open to broader viewpoints that take in more of *the* truth.

### Trap Overlap

There is overlap among the traps I've just shared. It is likely you have more than one trap affecting you right now. If I were sitting beside you, we could have a real conversation about the traps, one that would challenge you to think about the grip they have on you. So now is the time for you to challenge yourself and examine how these traps are affecting you.

Because of this, we are not addressing the traps one by one. I prefer to roll them together and focus on how you can move forward from where you are right now, with the ultimate goal of finding your new path— one that combines exponential success with significance.

### Success Breeds Complacency

Safety is the enemy of success. There is a huge difference between starting a business and keeping it growing. It takes different skills and even different thinking. You can say the same for any professional endeavor.

Let's look at the beginnings of an entrepreneurial venture. Starting out, businesses can grow simply by executing on a good idea. It takes hard work, and it takes courage to overcome the challenges that come up. That is the typical path; while some take longer to make it, many never make it all.

For the few that turn the corner to profitability and larger scale, things can go one of two ways. They either continue to evolve or they don't. You can say the same for leaders—they either evolve or they don't.

Do you remember Kodak? Blockbuster? Circuit City? Borders Books? Those companies didn't make it for a number of reasons, but if we simplify it, they failed to stay relevant to consumers. They didn't evolve.

Meanwhile, companies like Apple and Amazon have navigated many market changes. Apple completely cannibalized its highest-margin product, the iPod, when it launched the iPhone. That worked out pretty well for them. Amazon has continued to grow far beyond books, such that now it's a colossus in online retail, cloud computing, and more.

There are many stories on both sides of success that we can look at. In the rest of this book, I will talk about a few other companies, but most of the examples will be about people. That's because I want to address you at a personal level. *Your* success. *Your* continuous growth. And, of course, *your* shift from conventional, linear success to exponential success and significance.

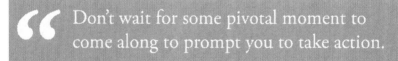

**"** Don't wait for some pivotal moment to come along to prompt you to take action.

### Don't Wait
This book is meant to activate you to step up *now*.

Don't wait for some pivotal moment to come along to prompt you to take action.

Don't fail to evolve, like so many businesses have done.

## THE TRAP OF SUCCESS

Don't let your fear kill your dreams or rob you of what you really want; show the courage to create a new future.

That new future is one where you regularly venture outside your comfort zone, where you achieve exponential success, and where you achieve deep significance in your work and life. To get there, you must listen to the calling in your soul.

That calling can be hard to hear. Maybe you don't hear it at all yet, but you will. At first, I ignored my calling. Maybe it was only a whisper. But by ignoring it I missed the signs of my true potential. It took me years of frustration and then years of new learning—the learning I'm sharing with you now—to hear my calling and begin to pursue it. It has made all the difference in my work and my life; I just wish I hadn't waited so long to find it.

Will you ignore your calling?

### Oprah's View of Success

Striving for success usually means making more money, having more freedom, maybe grabbing some fame. Yet those things often feel empty once you have attained them. That's what happened to me, and I've seen it happen with many others.

Oprah Winfrey says that she sees success as more than money and fame. It is about service. Her view of success takes it far beyond the ego. This is Oprah's prayer that she borrowed from Rev. Martin Luther King:

*"Use me, God. Show me how to take who I am, who I want to be, and what I can do, and use it for a purpose greater than myself."*

*That* is a calling. Yes, Oprah has money and fame—more than most people can imagine—but she has also been on a journey of significance for years as she has evolved in her career. Oprah has invited the dance of success and significance into her life, which is obvious when you see how she continuously shares with her audience after her show is long gone.

## For the Love of Money

Here is just one example of the limitations of conventional success from the crazy world of Wall Street. You may not have heard of Sam Polk, but his story is quite interesting. You'll likely enjoy it—if you're already thinking that success in life might be about more than just money.

Sam was a Wall Street investment banker at a top firm. It was a dream come true for him to work among the other traders, and he made more money in a year than most people make in a lifetime. He became driven by the money and the perks of life as a trader, pushing himself in nearly every area of life. Unfortunately, his never-ending drive was of the addict's variety—the same compulsion that had earlier pushed him into areas like alcohol, drugs, and overeating.

It all came to a head in 2014, when Sam received a bonus of $3.75 million. His hunger for more was obsessive, yet he realized that the path he was on was not the way he wanted to continue. Sam quit his high-paying Wall Street job and began a search for something more. I discovered an abridged version of Sam's story in a New York Times article, but you can read more about it—and his successful quest to find work of real significance—in his book, *For the Love of Money.*

## It's Not That Your Success Is Bad

Please understand: I'm not saying that traditional success is a bad thing. I'm also not saying it's a good thing. I'm only saying that there is more to life—and there must be more to your work—than the traditional pursuit of money and other shallow measures of success.

I've been on that treadmill. Having made tons of money in the first decade of this century, I felt the inner drive to make even more— even as I felt an emptiness in my stomach that ached for something meaningful in life. I realize now that what I wanted was significance. I wanted to escape my own trap of success.

Like me or like Sam Polk, you might be on a similar path that will cause you to look back at your life, or parts of it, with regret. My hope is that this book will give you a new perspective on success and significance, one that will encourage you to continue to grow and innovate as you navigate life.

Getting there is about working on yourself, not about shortcuts or even "strategies." It requires building your self-awareness, and especially your awareness of what you really want out of life, and how that aligns or contrasts with how you're actually running your career.

I believe that facing this challenge is 80 percent mindset and 20 percent mechanics. The lion's share of our success is about the way you think—what I sometimes refer to as the "inner game." If all you focus on is traditional success, you can attain it with the right strategies and enough hard work, courage, and resilience. It's no easy task—but it also doesn't answer your inner needs. So before you go any further down that road, ask yourself, "What do I really want?"

Do you just want more money? Or do you really want something else? Something deeper?

If you're reading this book, I assume you want more than money. So it's time to start learning how to reinvent yourself.

### Questions to Inspire You

1. Has your personal idea of success changed over time? What was it five years ago?
2. What is your idea of success now?
3. Do you want to pursue your true calling? Do you even know what it is? Will you ignore it or embrace it?
4. What do you want? Really want?

Thank you for reading!

Dear Reader,

I hope you are enjoying The Trap of Success. This project was extremely difficult for me to write. I wanted to bare my soul to you to share the struggles and doubt that I endured so you can make some new decisions and take new actions that will create a business (and life) of significance. Each chapter going forward played a central part in my own personal growth and my journey to significance.

Also, I hope that this book will engage you in new strategies that will fuel your profound success. Thank you for spending your time soaking it all in.

Finally, I need to ask you a favor. If you're enjoying the book, I'd love a review of The Trap of Success on Amazon. You can find my book here:
http://thetrapofsuccess.com/review

Thanks in advance,

PS. Thank you so much for reading this book and for all the work that you WILL do to make this book valuable to you. Keep reading...it only gets better from here.

# REINVENTING YOURSELF

"

And when I say, life does not happen to you, it happens for you, I really don't know if that is true. I'm making a conscious choice to perceive challenges as something of benefit. So I can deal with them the most productive way.

-Jim Carrey, Actor and Funny Man

## THE TRAP OF SUCCESS

I was alone with my thoughts. It was 9:57 p.m., and I was consumed with doubt and fear. That's not normal for me: I have a positive outlook on the world around me and usually look for the happy parts of life. However, at that moment, all I could focus on was what was *not* going well. I thought about the pressure of making money and making a difference. I thought about my health, and the extra 20 pounds of flab I've carried with me for the past decade (well, really more like 17 years).

In that moment, I thought of my wife and our relationship. We have been married for nearly 14 years and, as with any marriage, we have seen our highs and lows.

I started to focus on what was going on with us—all through a negative filter—until my doubt reached a point of confusion. My wife was visiting her mother in Alabama for the weekend. She had taken our son so I could get some work done on this book.

To give you an idea of what put me in that place, let me share with you what I had been doing that led to that moment. I had spent the day writing about fear and doubt for this very book. You'll get there in the chapter on "Leaning into Fear." As you'll hear me say more than once, you get more of whatever you focus on. If you focus on fear, you will evoke fear in your life. You will begin to see things to be afraid of. You will find ways to doubt yourself. It's a cycle of life that I have seen happen over and over.

It is embarrassing for me to even tell you, but I had worked myself up into a crisis of doubt. I called my wife's cell phone. We chatted about small stuff, and then I brought up the heavy subject of my fears. I told her that working on the book had caused me to find and analyze everything I could doubt about us. I kind of felt like I was losing my mind.

My wife responded, "Everything is great. What is wrong with you?"

I didn't really have an answer. I hung up the phone and began to cry.

Among the many thoughts in my mind, the main one was that she didn't understand me. I let the pain course through me, and with tears streaming down my face I grabbed a pad of paper to collect my thoughts. I wrote about our relationship, being a father, being a son, even my personal health.

I wanted to change everything I could in that moment. I kept writing down different areas that needed an overhaul to create the life I wanted.

Writing this book was causing me to think about things I had repressed for years. My reflections were more acute because I was reaching a new phase in my life that would require me to show up differently and to be more intentional, and that reality unearthed a lot of fears. I don't normally repress things, but most of this was so dark and scary, deep down inside me, that I wanted to keep it hidden from everyone.

And now I realized that it was not helping me to keep it pushed down. I needed to accept that change was necessary, and not just a small change, but a *reinvention*.

## Confronting the Need for Change

Let's look at what happens when you decide to take on a new project in your work or business. Assume it's something you've never done before, like I'm doing in writing this kind of book.

As I've discovered, when you're writing a book, you will eventually meet with resistance. For me, it didn't happen right away, but my doubts began to build as I got beyond the planning phases.

To be clear, this wasn't about not knowing what to do. I had done about a dozen interviews with editors, friends who have written books, and guests on my podcast who had experience in this area. Plus I had collaborated on other books (much drier, research-based ones) early in my career, so it's not as though I was entering this world unprepared.

On top of that, I have been living through the lessons I'm sharing in this book for twenty years. And yet I still began to encounter resistance as I got deeper into the drafting process. The act of writing it all down in an organized way forced me to undergo a process of deep personal reevaluation. And that resistance was followed by doubt.

Now, if you are a natural at writing books and never went through that period of doubt...then you suck. (Just kidding—sort of.)

What I discovered in all the conversations I had with authors— and we're talking about New York Times best-sellers here—is that the process of writing that first book, and even the following books, is just *hard*.

But if you're committed, and if you're willing to get uncomfortable and to grow, something happens inside you. As you sit with being uncomfortable, you come to a choice. You can either let the resistance stop you, or you can decide to keep going. For me, I chose to be insanely curious about what happens when you keep going.

I dug deep to get behind the resistance. I looked beneath the surface to find out what was really going on inside me.

There were more barriers to overcome. As I poured myself into the writing, I began to make up stories in my head about the value of my journey and even other aspects of my life. These stories grew to take over my thinking, and they threatened to stop me from writing more.

One example is my doubt in my core story that I've already shared with you—about losing millions and then finding my path through the darkness to make my comeback. I have told that story hundreds of times in private conversations and on public stages. But before I did, I had to make it through a crucial turning point that came about two months after losing those millions.

At that time, I was really considering the coaching profession. I wanted to help others make their own transformations. But I felt deep anguish about others accepting me as their business coach. The thought of being a coach to business leaders right after being the guy who lost everything was scary. But I had to wrestle my fears and get over that anguish so I could progress.

As I got deeper into the coaching world, I learned to share my journey. I have never been shy about telling what happened to me, inside and out, because of my business ordeal. But my inner voice would whisper to me "This story again? When are you going to let it go?" I struggled with that for what seems like decades, even though it has been only seven years since the "2x4 day." This doubt still comes up from time to time, yet I keep telling my story because who knows who will benefit from my pain.

*But what if I had let fear stop me?*

What would I have then? You wouldn't be holding this book, for sure. You would likely not know who I am and you wouldn't have a chance to read about creating significance in your world. You wouldn't know about mastering the dance of success and significance that runs through this book.

Sometimes the stories in our head stop us. In fact, I stopped writing the book for about six weeks even though I didn't want to change the publish date.

I can smile about it now, because I've come to believe that I needed to go through that period of uncertainty so I could face the challenge of reinventing myself and then complete the book. I had to do it so I could bring this book to you. I wanted you to be able to read it and use it to create the dance of success and significance in your life. But I also had to do it for me.

This project forced me to grow. It was challenging, and I know that the growth has been essential for more than just the book. I had to reinvent other aspects of my life that were out of alignment with my true identity. I changed the way I eat and care for my health. And I changed the way I think about some deeply personal issues that have put me on a path to a new identity—a better version of myself that fits my own quest for significance and exponential success.

The process led me to analyze all aspects of my life. I looked at areas that I had been afraid to change for decades—areas where I had made excuses and, frankly, accepted that a limited version of myself was "just who I am."

I'm sharing this part of the story with you because it was a very real struggle that I endured while writing this book, and it may parallel what you experience—what I've seen so many others experience—as you encounter something truly **new** in your life.

## My Reinvention: Influence, Impact, and Income

When I'm on stage, I often talk about the three commonly known *I's* of marketing: influence, impact, and income. Very simply, to create more *income*, you have to create *impact* in the lives of others, and to create impact, you have to exert a certain level of *influence*. These three *I's* are a useful lens for looking at your professional and personal growth.

However, there is a fourth *"I"* that belongs here: *"Identity."* What I mean by Identity is how you see yourself. How you see your role in this world. If you have a warped or limited view of your identity, as I realized I did in the process of writing this book, it will be hard for you to create something you've never created before.

This is really the hard part: you have to be willing to change your identity to meet new and bigger challenges in your life.

What you already understand and what you have already done to create success in your life is exactly what is keeping you from creating significance and achieving exponential success. In other words, you have to be willing to reinvent your identity to achieve next-level growth.

## Your Strategy Must Change

I'm not saying that your current strategy to grow as a person or to grow your business is wrong. Who am I to say that without knowing you?

If you believe that you have the right strategy already in place to create exponential success, and then by following it you also work your way to significance, that's great.

However, I have seen that many people get extremely complacent by "doing it the way they've always done it." They focus on what has worked in the past and simply do more of that—even when it's *not* bringing them greater success or significance. (Think of the four different traps from the last chapter: the thread that runs through them is over-connection to your status quo.)

If you are willing to look at yourself from a different perspective from time to time, it can bring you exponential growth, especially if you have been living within self-imposed barriers. Thinking that you already have the right strategy might be exactly what is holding you back.

Look at your beliefs. Look for new ways to spark higher creativity and innovation. Choose to be insanely curious about what you haven't already tried. This applies to anything you are aiming to create in your life.

 If you are not willing to disrupt yourself in the business world, someone else will do it for you.

You may not realize it, but you might have been sabotaging yourself all this time. You may have been accepting the idea that what has created conventional success for you in the past is going to be your path to exponential success and significance. But why would that make sense? It's like the old saying goes: if you do what you have always done, you will get what you have always gotten.

## THE TRAP OF SUCCESS

I had the pleasure to interview Ryan Estis, a professional speaker to the corporate market, on my podcast. He sees the idea of success and reinvention from a perspective similar to mine. I love these words from Ryan:

*"Success breeds complacency. Disrupt yourself before the market does it for you."*
-**Ryan Estis,** Energetic Speaker and Leader of Leaders

If you are not willing to disrupt yourself in the business world, someone else will do it for you.

This leads us to a vital lesson: what you believe right now might not be the truth.

### Your Truth vs. The Truth

There is a difference between "your truth" and "the truth." You are focused on your goals. Your income. Your learning. Don't get me wrong—each of these is extremely important. But they are based on what you believe.

We often hold what we *believe* as THE truth. Yet we rarely think about or challenge what we believe. We just accept it as the way it is. This is normal, because you have experiences and even data to back up your beliefs. That's how your mind works.

There is a difference, though, between your truth and the absolute truth.

Your truth operates when you create stories that allow you to understand the world. Those stories become your guides to the future. You start to look for them in the world, focusing on evidence and narratives that reinforce those stories. The stories become integral to the way you see yourself, your future, and your path to success and significance, so you interpret the world based on them.

However, those stories are something that you yourself made up. They are not the way that everyone sees the world, nor should they be. They are also prone to confirmation bias, in which you selectively ignore contradictory evidence and cherry-pick the reasoning that supports what you already believe and already know—or think you know.

Think of some of the beliefs and meanings that you accept as a given. It might be your view that working in sales is slimy. Or that marketing is manipulative. Or that you're not worthy of success. Yes, I know it's a big jump to the concept of "worthiness," but I want to get your attention about how important this is.

What if the story you've been holding so dear is just something that you made up? Yes, it is your truth, but that means it's just another example of the way you see the world. It is not the absolute truth. Here, I'm referring to "absolute truth" as something that is verifiable by others, not something based only on your opinion.

What I'm getting at is this: the stories that you carry with you shape how you see the world and how you see yourself.

In other words, your truth can hold you back from having what you really want, if it's keeping you from seeing what's truly possible outside your old assumptions and beliefs.

I thought I would help you to see the three beliefs (a.k.a. "My Truths") that I had to let go of to reinvent myself. These are mine, and yours are likely different. But my hope is that you can read these and then be inspired to uncover your truths that you've been carrying around. Deeper into this chapter I will share how to reframe your truths. Reframing will allow you to gain a new perspective on your current beliefs.

## Letting Go of My Truths

In my journey to significance, I had to question my story of life, and the truths that I had accepted as "just the way life is." I could not have reinvented myself without going through this process.

57

## THE TRAP OF SUCCESS

The three truths that follow were ingrained in me over years. I could have told you many stories and presented carefully selected data to support my beliefs. Yet to grow as a person and find what I was seeking in life, I had to question these fundamental truths and then adapt them.

### #1 Success is measured by the size of our bank accounts.

Before my "2x4 day" I had plenty of money and a cash-cow business—what we think of as "financial security." Looking back after all that happened, I can see that I suffered from a form of greed.

There are different kinds of greed. My own kind caused me to always strive for more money and growth in my business and then to save that money for the future. It may not sound like a problem, but greed governed my day-to-day thoughts. This obsession also shaped how I spent money: for example, I took ages to make big purchases in my personal life.

Greed led me to stay in a business that caused me pain, one that I complained about constantly, because I couldn't imagine going without that financial security.

I let my obsession with money pull me away from my relationships in life and allowed it to over-inflate my sense of importance. During that period of my life, I became so self-involved that sometimes I felt like I was living like a professional athlete: I wanted my wife to anticipate my needs to keep me sharp for my work. I am ashamed to admit it, but during those times I thought that I was more important than my wife. It damaged our relationship, which I am frankly still working to repair. Fortunately, we love each other very much.

When I lost it all and had to reinvent myself, I had to change the way I thought about money, and by extension the way I thought about myself. After plenty of soul-searching, I made some huge changes. The main one was that I decided to focus on making a difference for others first, and trust that the money would flow from there. This was hardly an overnight change—it took time and careful moves to make it happen—but today I *don't* focus on money.

58

What about you? What is your truth around money?

Do you focus on it so much that you miss other opportunities? Or make damaging tradeoffs like I did?

Are you holding on to a truth about money that can be challenged?

Money is essential to businesses, and to life in general. Therefore it's very likely that you will struggle with the meaning you give to money, as I did, on your journey of self-reinvention.

### #2 Failure is not an option.

You have heard these exact words before—maybe most famously in Ed Harris's portrayal of NASA Flight Director Gene Kranz in the film *Apollo 13*. I myself have said them many times in the past. To me, this mantra was part of my hard-driving need to succeed. I have always created the life and business I wanted. In fact, the notion of creating what I want is still a core belief for me.

However, in the past I had a personal feeling that failure would mean the end of everything. I logically knew that failure is a chance to learn, but that's not the way I felt about it deep inside. In fact, the fear of failure is what kept me from pivoting my sports tour business into something else. I was afraid to fail and lose what I had created.

Looking back now allows me to see what was really going on with me. I was so determined to grow my company that I could not see that I should have been chasing a completely different goal. In picking up the pieces of my life after the collapse of my business, I had to look at failure in new ways. I had to challenge those old beliefs.

I started to see the value in failure as a part of successful living. I was able to let myself see the learning moments that arise out of failure. When I think back about that "2x4 day," I have mixed feelings. I wish I could have learned the lessons I got from that experience without actually going through it. I wish I could have grown without having lost millions and impacted so many friends and customers.

59

## THE TRAP OF SUCCESS

Once I worked through my failure issues, I started to see the value in living full-out. I saw the importance of being vulnerable when going after new goals. I started investing in myself again and putting projects together that would drive me to a new future.

What is your truth around failure?

Looking back at times where you didn't get what you expected, how long did it take you before getting back on your feet? Did you understand the lessons that you were meant to learn from your failures?

### #3 There are different kinds of forgiveness.
This is a BIG one—one that I struggled with through many, many months of introspection.

About six months after the "2x4 day," I began to think about how to forgive the person who took my money and my business from me. I had studied forgiveness in my coach training. I remembered an old saying about forgiveness. Its origins are obscure, but it's been cited by everyone from Nelson Mandela to Alcoholics Anonymous:

*"Not forgiving someone is like drinking poison and expecting the other person to die."*

Looking at this quote makes me laugh now. It is so true that the energy drain and stress that keeping someone on your "never forgive" list is similar to taking poison for yourself.

Six months after, I talked with my wife about my need to forgive the person who caused my "2x4 day." She thought I was out of my mind. Well, she actually shared a few four-letter words with me about this "great" idea of mine. My wife had endured the whole ordeal with me and suffered just like I had. Her thoughts, at that time, were about revenge, not forgiveness. The impulse to exact revenge is a common tendency among all people. How can you forgive someone who put you through this? I won't tell you the ideas that friends and even strangers have shared with me about retaliation.

But I knew that I needed to find forgiveness so I could move on. As I struggled with it, I realized that I could forgive the perpetrator later. Meanwhile, I worked with my coach at the time, Charles Feltman, who led me through a series of questions, each of which was powerful enough to force me to look at things from a new perspective.

Through that work with Charles, I began to reframe what I needed. I came up with a powerfully simple change. Charles helped me make a grounded decision to table the question of forgiveness for one year. I know it sounds so simple. But, honestly, this experience showed me the power of learning through coaching. I needed to forgive—it was the key to my emotional freedom and being able to move forward with a new clarity. But I also needed to give myself enough time to get there.

Over time, I started to see it all quite differently. I began to think about how the forgiveness I needed was not for the other person. I needed forgiveness *for me*. I needed to forgive myself for trusting my friend. I needed to forgive myself for all the pain. The release that came with those truths was a pivotal moment in my life. I would not be where I am today if I had continued to blame myself and harbor the pain of that whole experience.

What is your truth around forgiveness?

What is your understanding of forgiveness?

Who do you need to forgive? Is it you?

## Shifting Your Beliefs

We all have different versions of the truth that we hold on to. Some of those may help us, but some may hurt us. I shared three of my own truths that needed to be challenged. The key to doing this for yourself is separating your *belief* (your truth) from the absolute truth. It might not be easy, but it is worth it.

What is your truth? Which illusions and preconceptions do you need to let go of to find the absolute truth?

61

## THE TRAP OF SUCCESS

Now we can look at how to use these truths—your own truths that you have examined and challenged—to reinvent yourself. This doesn't start with *doing*. It starts with your *being*.

*"One of the most important parts of being a leader is to look in the mirror and tell the truth about what you are seeing. Even if—especially if—it's not good."*
-**Adam Braun**, Founder of Pencils of Promise and Changemaker

Looking in the mirror is something most of us do every day. However, you take for granted who is looking back at you. You justify, and make excuses for yourself. That is the problem, but it also contains the seeds of the solution.

### Reinvention Comes from the Inside

When you see your beliefs through a new lens, you can start to make changes. In fact, change won't happen until you achieve that new understanding. You must be aware of the problem before you can address it.

I mentioned Rich Litvin in Chapter 2. Rich shared with me how even the most successful people tend to opt for their status quo. In other words, they don't really change, even though they want to. They keep falling back into the old patterns.

Here is a quote from Rich that paints a picture for the most powerful force that exists between a coach and a client:

*"There's only one thing more powerful than you when speaking to a potential client. And there's only one thing more powerful than the potential client in front of you. And that's the status quo."*
—**Rich Litvin**, Co-Author of The Prosperous Coach and Master Coach

People are programmed to look for what science refers to as *homeostasis*. In science, homeostasis is the tendency of the body to seek and maintain a condition of balance or equilibrium in its internal environment, even when faced with external changes. A simple example of homeostasis is the body's ability to maintain an internal temperature around 98.6 degrees Fahrenheit, whatever the temperature outside.

As this relates to you and reinvention, homeostasis is the pull to remain the same, to stay on the same narrow path. You can easily see this when people diet. For 99 percent of the people who have ever tried to change their eating habits, homeostasis is the body's desire to remain at the same weight, even if that means changing your metabolism to hold on to fat. The body fights your changes to keep its fat stores, unless you break through that barrier.

On your journey to creating a new way of living and seeing the world, you will run up against homeostasis again and again. It is a natural drive to keep things the same as they have always been in an effort to keep us safe. Your body and mind will try to stop change and keep you right where you are, even if it is not good for you.

## Breaking Away From the Status Quo

Making a deep change will always start from the inside. That applies just as much to breaking free from your comfort zone to get new results as it does to any diet you start.

What I mean by "the inside" is your thinking. This is your inner game... your mindset...your beliefs...your thoughts...your ideas.

Really, we're talking about your subconscious mind—the part of the brain that operates at the deepest level of your being. It processes and filters the world you see. Your subconscious imposes its limitations on you and keeps you from creating the change you seek.

## How to Reinvent Yourself

Your job is to challenge those beliefs. Question them and doubt them. The main problem that keeps us stuck in homeostasis and prevents us from reinvention is our subconscious emotional attachment to our own way—to the status quo. We put blinders on that prevent us from even *seeing* other options.

## THE TRAP OF SUCCESS

That's why the process of challenging your beliefs is easier to undertake with a trained mentor or coach. I didn't understand this until I became a coach in 2010. Now, after thousands of coaching interactions with people, I see it so clearly in the way people continue to behave in just the same ways even when they want to get very different new results.

One simple way to challenge your current beliefs—a method I use with my own clients—is to develop multiple options for a given solution. Push yourself to think of ideas you have never considered before. Look to others you know who are trying unique approaches. Gather your list of options and begin challenging them.

Once you have some options to choose from, I invite you to look at them differently than before. Look at the beliefs and assumptions you've held onto that have not allowed you to see something as a viable strategy before. Look at the emotions each of these assumptions stirs up inside you. Are you willing to get uncomfortable while assessing the options? In my years of coaching, I have found that people have often avoided very good strategies just because of the need to be comfortable. That's why I wrote Chapter 7, "Getting Uncomfortable."

If you struggle to come up with options or different perspectives for finding solutions, then you really need to talk to someone about it. My suggestion is to reach out to someone who has overcome barriers similar to yours and achieved aims similar to your own. That is the external approach that I outline in Chapter 8, "Leaning into Fear."

We all have different truths—beliefs, assumptions—that must be faced as we reinvent ourselves. Many of them are small and hard to see. These ideas are subtle to us and maybe even invisible to others. Keep working with your truths as you take the journey to significance.

In the meantime, here is a story of someone I admire who had to change the way he saw the world. He had to wrestle with beliefs and truths that were very deeply ingrained in his thinking.

## From Incarceration to Reinvention

I could share many personal stories or client examples here that embody the resistance to new ways of seeing reality. Instead, I want to share a story about Mike Pisciotta's incarceration and reinvention.

Mike, another guest on my podcast, found himself at a crossroads in life at the age of 18. He went on a bender of sorts; there were drinks and there were pills. Next thing he knew, he woke up in a jail cell. Waking up behind bars and not really remembering what he did that landed him there, Mike looked over his life and the decisions that he was making. The long and short of it is that he had two real choices. He could continue on a path of substance abuse and crime. Or he could change everything he knew about himself and clean up his act.

It may be easy for you to say that he had only one real choice. However, the reality is that some people are okay with jail. They don't want to be in the real world. And some people don't want to change their ways.

Before even going to trial for his actions, Mike had made his decision. You can probably guess that I selected this story to share with you because it has a happy ending. But if Mike hadn't acknowledged that he did have a choice and then made the right decision, he wouldn't have anything.

Today, Mike runs an online marketing business called Marketing Your Purpose. To get where he is, Mike went through many iterations of wrestling with his truth. He had to challenge his beliefs about the world and himself, understanding that they were not absolute. Mike made a commitment that, no matter what happened in court or even during his sentence, he would reinvent himself.

Mike used his period of incarceration to learn business and a new language. He chose to use his time wisely and make an impact in the world because he wanted significance. Mike's journey embodies one of my main points, too: there is a dance between success and significance. Mike found that out by creating his business. His way to success has been to embrace significance, too.

## THE TRAP OF SUCCESS

### Your Shift

My hope is that you can see more about yourself through Mike's story, even though his experiences were extreme. You don't have to lose everything like I did, or go to jail like Mike did, to commit to reinvent yourself.

Keep in mind that if you *don't* have such an extreme experience, it might even be harder for you to see the need for a change. As I said, some of your truths will be subtle and hidden from you, or even impossible for you to see. And that is exactly the problem.

Have you built up walls that keep you from seeing yourself in new ways?

Do you see new choices for yourself?

If you want to change something in your life or business, you will need to find those new choices.

### How to Reframe

There are times when you have to look at the beliefs you hold onto and change them using a technique called "reframing." Reframing is a process of changing the meaning, or context, that someone assigns to a situation or belief.

It starts by accepting that humans organize every single thing in life, starting in childhood, by assigning a meaning to it. We attach meaning to the things that happen to us and to others. We remember those formative moments and often refuse to let go of them. Some of them are small, while others are large and obviously vital to our lives moving forward. I have talked with many people who have childhood memories that are packed away inside them. They carry these memories throughout life. We all do.

Memories like those have caused you to guide your life toward or away from different areas. Not all of these memories are bad for you. Some have made you courageous and strong in your life. However, some have also caused you to limit your growth because of the emotional connections that you have assigned to them.

One example from business is the way you think about *sales*. Many people have the belief that sales is slimy. It is a meaning they have associated with selling, usually because of how someone sold to them—or pressured them—before. This makes them feel uneasy about situations in which *they* need to do the selling, which is a belief that keeps many entrepreneurs from growing their businesses. They wait for clients to come to them and do the asking.

When I encounter this resistance to selling with my clients, I rely on reframing their view of sales. The first—and usually the only—strategy I use is to ask them about the value of their services. If they can "own" their value to their clients, then they can reframe selling away from feeling slimy and toward providing that value. Understanding in a deep way that what you do is valuable and provides real results to your clients allows you to reframe any negative beliefs about selling.

In general, the shift takes their thinking from "Selling is something you do *to* someone" to "Selling is something you do *for* someone." This kind of reframing is usually easy to do and can be applied to many areas of growth. Selling is just the tip of the iceberg.

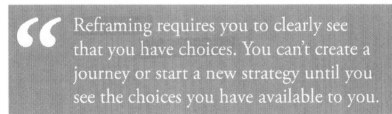

> Reframing requires you to clearly see that you have choices. You can't create a journey or start a new strategy until you see the choices you have available to you.

If that example seems too simple or easy, let's look at a much harder example of reframing that had incredibly powerful emotions attached. In this case, a young mother who lost a child was able to move forward after years of grief.

67

## THE TRAP OF SUCCESS

I witnessed this life-changing transformation during my coach training in 2010, when my fellow student Natalie Pere was in the coaching program with me. I want to thank her for letting me share this very personal story with you here.

During a group coaching session, the coach and Natalie were surrounded by more than 50 students. No one had any idea what was going to be discussed.

The session started off as expected with the coach asking, "How do you want to use our time today?" The conversation wandered a bit until Natalie mentioned the pain that she still held inside from losing her baby more than a decade earlier.

The room was deathly quiet as the coach helped Natalie explore this sensitive part of her history. I remember the tears flowing down my face as her story unfolded. The experience stirred everyone in the room.

Then the the coach asked, "What is the real issue here?"

Natalie said, "I will never forget my baby. Even though everyone tells me to forgive and move on."

The coach probed deeper to figure out what was happening inside Natalie's thinking. Finally it was uncovered: Natalie had a belief that "forgiveness" and "forgetting" were linked together. The conversation reached its crescendo when Natalie realized that she could see the two as being separate. She didn't have to forget her baby to forgive herself for what had happened.

The coach worked with Natalie to reframe her beliefs so she could forgive herself without ever needing to forget the death of her baby. Natalie had the choice to continue with a coupled definition, or to move ahead with a new perspective that separated "forgiveness" from "forgetting." That allowed her to change the meaning that she had assigned to her baby's death for all those years.

When I followed up with Natalie six years later, she said to me, "That conversation opened up so much for me and the path that I continue on. I am still unraveling layers of shame, accompanied by forgiveness and compassion. The light is revealed in our darkest moments."

If reframing can work in a case as profound as that one, it can be applied in many other situations when you are stuck, or when you are determined that you want to change but aren't sure what is holding you back from making decisions.

Reframing requires you to clearly see that you have choices. You can't create a journey or start a new strategy until you see the choices you have available to you.

### Getting to Choice

Having options laid out before you is really a beautiful thing. Having options puts you in the driver's seat; you have control. It is what I call "getting to choice."

You'll notice I am sharing many people's stories with you throughout this book. I encourage you to reflect on each one to see how I've clearly defined the choice that each person made so they could move forward.

I opened this chapter with a quote from Jim Carrey. I reprint it here to point something out.

*"And when I say, life does not happen to you, it happens for you, I really don't know if that is true. I'm making a conscious choice to perceive challenges as something of benefit. So I can deal with them the most productive way."*
—**Jim Carrey,** Actor and Funny Man

Carrey starts by realizing that he has a choice. Even when he was a young unknown, he didn't accept that he was adrift in life. Even today, he wants to be intentional about why he chooses one way or another.

## THE TRAP OF SUCCESS

Once you realize that you have choices—that you don't have to just follow the well-worn path—you are in the position for reinvention. This is a glorious thing. When you "get to choice," it means you can choose to stay the same or you can choose to change.

In coaching, one of the most powerful aspects of the relationship comes in the moments when a client realizes that they are "at choice." And they can then choose a new way of being, a new way of showing up. This is one of the reasons why I feel significance in what I do—having deep conversations with clients about things they have never uttered to another person, and getting them to see that they can make a different decision with real control over their life. They are clear about the options, the possibilities, and the consequences.

As a coach, the best option in those moments is to bite my tongue and let the silence do the work. The silence becomes leverage to prompt a decision. Frankly, the silence is uncomfortable, but it creates the space for the client to ponder and brood over their choices. This is the very moment when clients get to embrace directions that are new and, likely, bold. And the bigger the decision, the longer the silence.

When you realize that you have choices, you can change your life in a moment, with a single decision.

### Making It Stick
Making anything stick takes commitment and discipline. But it doesn't stop there. You need to have the right strategy, develop the right practices, and remain persistent.

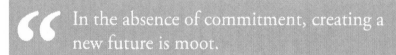

> **In the absence of commitment, creating a new future is moot.**

You have to make a commitment to overcome the pull of homeostasis or the status quo. You can look ahead to Chapter 10, "Playing to Win," to see more about that kind of commitment.

In the absence of commitment, creating a new future is moot.

I feel that most people don't really understand "commitment." For too many of them, the word means "I will do it if it is easy or convenient." Well, let me tell you a secret: the path to significance is rarely going to be easy and convenient. In fact, it is likely to challenge you in ways that you have never thought of.

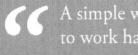 A simple way to look at it is this: you have to work harder on yourself than the things on your to-do list.

Beyond that, making your reinvention stick is more about your own personal identity. If you can't shed the vision of the "old" you, you will struggle. But if you are willing to go deep and uncover the real issues, you have a fighting chance.

It is hard work to become self-aware. That hard work will always be something you must welcome as you grow, develop, and change.

A simple way to look at it is this: you have to work harder on yourself than the things on your to-do list.

### Aligning the Outside with the Inside

Here is a question to ponder: how are you showing up?

This is a deep question if you look beyond the surface level of your clothes, shoes, and even your hair. It is not about being punctual, either.

When I say "showing up," I mean your internal self. It shows up in the posture of your body and even the language you use, but those things reflect your thinking, your attitude, and your self-worth.

Let's look at one piece here: your body language. Showing up slumped and closed off will immediately signal to the world that something isn't right. Bouncing into a room with tons of energy and a smile that you can't wipe off—you tell the world a different story.

Think of how you read body language in others. You know, for instance, that crossed arms are a signal of resistance or detachment. You have been reading others your whole life, looking for signs in body language and making judgments in microseconds. Did you know that your own body communicates with others in a similar way?

On top of that, your physical posture affects your own moods and emotions. In fact, I can make a case that your posture is connected to all parts of you and how you show up.

Now, think about your choice of language. Your language includes both your word choice and your tone. Are you using words of doubt, or confidence? Of resistance, or purpose? Your language is another indicator of how you think on the inside.

A common example here is the often stated, "I must do _____." Fill in the blank as you choose. The key is the word "must." If you live in a place where you have rules that say you "must" do something, you are operating out of some obligation. However, by switching your language to "get to," you change the power of the sentence.

Try it. Say "I must clean the house." It's probably something you say often and certainly something I hope you do often. But now say "I get to clean the house." This comes from a place of gratitude. Can you feel it when you make this small change? You do have to really say the words out loud to make this work. Try it.

My intention here is to help you be more aware of your words and your body. When you can do that, you are much more likely to make the inner shift required for reinvention. That's because reinvention requires looking at the way you engage with all of life—your emotions, the tone of your voice, your word choices, and your body language. In fact, I would even say that you *cannot* make a complete change on the inside without it showing up on the outside. Everything is connected.

Once you start paying attention to how you are showing up, you can make conscious decisions about your posture, your facial expressions, and your language. All of these come from the inside, but sometimes we forget to align the outside to the inside.

## Embracing Your Evolution

Change is not something you can avoid. You can try. You can resist it. You can fight it with all your might. But at some point you will realize that it is a losing battle. Change is continuous.

Life evolves. You must evolve, too. The art of reinventing yourself is necessary for meeting new challenges.

In moments of crisis and, more importantly, in the everyday moments of your life, you *can* reinvent yourself—if you choose to. I shared the story of my own reinvention, which came on the heels of losing millions. I shared Mike Pisciotta's story of reinvention through going to jail. However, your reinvention may be harder. I say this because the trap of success is nearly invisible. It may seem that all is well, yet something inside you struggles with what *could* be.

Your strategy must change if you want to pursue the dance of significance. The beliefs and truths that you hold dear must also change. As I've explained in this chapter, my own truths about money, failure, and forgiveness all had to change for me to find significance.

My claim is that it starts on the inside. It begins with your thinking, and it requires you to break the status quo. You may find the need to reframe stories in your life. And you will need to see clearly the choices you must make to move forward.

Remember, making your reinvention stick requires commitment—real commitment—along with aligning the new beliefs inside you with how you are showing up on the outside.

## THE TRAP OF SUCCESS

In the next chapter, I will lay out the principles of thinking bigger. Don't miss the lessons from a 3-foot-tall giant.

### Questions to Inspire You

1. Can you remember a moment that required you to reinvent yourself?
2. When have you reframed an old belief into a more powerful one, allowing you to accomplish something you've never done before?
3. What areas of your life and business need a reinvention now?

# THE PRINCIPLES OF THINKING BIGGER

Confidence is the
by-product of courage.

-Sean Stephenson, Powerful Speaker and
3-Foot-Tall Giant

## THE TRAP OF SUCCESS

The doctors told his parents that he was not expected to live beyond the first 24 hours. At his birth in 1979, it was discovered that he had a rare genetic disorder called osteogenesis imperfecta that made his bones so fragile they would break every time he sneezed. This is commonly referred to as "brittle bone disease." He had hundreds of bone fractures by age 17. With all that he endured, he learned to look at life as a gift instead of a burden.

If you don't know who I'm talking about, his name is Sean Stephenson. I started this chapter with a quote from him—the irony being that a chapter about thinking bigger centers on telling you how Sean, only three feet tall, sees life.

As a teenager, Sean heard the song "Hail to the Chief." He shared with me the thoughts he had then. Everyone stands for the President when he enters the room, and they clap for him, too. Sean said his thought at that moment was "What a cool job. I want to do that. I want to be President."

Okay, be honest, are you wondering how someone who is three feet tall and has extreme challenges in everyday functioning is going to be President of the United States? It doesn't make you odd to have those thoughts; in fact, it puts you in the majority. I smiled when he shared this story with me, kind of knowing that his dream of attaining the presidency is nearly impossible. Frankly, I get tired just thinking about the butts you have to kiss and the sacrifices you have to make to reach that goal regardless of who you are.

As a teenager, Sean faced many critics of his goal. He heard people that he trusted and loved tell him that it was impossible. Sean didn't accept their reality. Sean didn't listen to the critics.

My point here is to *ignore* your critics if you want to do something they don't understand. I don't care how much they love you and how "realistic" they think they are being. "Realistic" is just another word for "negative."

You can't listen to the people who don't empower you. People who label you only keep you down.

*"If you suck, keep sucking. Keep sucking until you don't suck anymore. Then you get better."*
—**Sean Stephenson**, Renowned Coach and Mentor

Holding on to his dream of reaching the Presidency, Sean strives to complete his real mission as an inspirational speaker. Ultimately, he wants to rid the world of insecurities. He uses his gift of speaking and his gift of his rare bone disorder to reach people all over the world, to inspire them to think bigger and get off their "buts." By the way, Sean's second book is titled *Get off Your "But."*

Despite Sean's challenges, he has taken a stand for others to shift their sense of self-worth. His work has reached millions of people around the world, including Sir Richard Branson, President Clinton, and the Dalai Lama. He has appeared on everything from Oprah to YouTube videos with millions of views. The Biography Channel did an hour-long feature on his life called "Three Foot Giant."

Sean's outlook on thinking bigger is powerful. He believes it is more important to *have* a dream than to achieve the dream. You get out of bed for a reason when you have a dream.

Sean made a huge discovery years back that enabled him to shift his view of success in the world. He stopped focusing on the money of his business. He now sees that his role is about significance; helping others see their real value in the world is his core focus. The business he runs now is in service of that mission. Sean told me, "I'm not here for me anymore. I am here for the human race."

And remember Sean's dream of becoming President of the United States? He has not made it yet. He is young. He has time. If he decides to make a shift into politics, he may yet be President. Indeed, Sean learned a lot about government when he interned for Bill Clinton during his time in office. If you ever have a chance to see Sean speak, consider yourself lucky to hear his story about him in his wheelchair being blown about on the lawn of the White House as Bill Clinton arrived via Marine One.

As you read the rest of this chapter, I want you to keep Sean's example in mind. He's a person who has every excuse you could imagine for not doing big things, yet he goes right ahead and dares to dream bigger than most people ever will. Before you go on, take a few minutes to answer these questions for yourself:

- What's your biggest dream? What scares you?
- Are you stuck in the comfort zone of GOOD?
- Is that preventing you from transforming into GREAT?

The enemy to getting what you want is your **comfort**. Being comfortable will kill your desire to be **great**.

In school, we're taught to conform. That's reinforced in the workplace. In many settings, we are rewarded for following the rules and getting in line with the goals of the organization. That kind of conformity may not be something you think about, but it plays within your mind when you decide you want to do something big.

### The Mindset of Thinking Bigger

One major problem with our world is that we don't think big enough to inspire us to make something seemingly impossible happen.

The people doing BIG things are likely no more capable than you. They're not necessarily smarter or blessed with more talent. They just decided to not let society keep them from creating the life they wanted. And the tribe of those creating significance is full of people who are doing what others said could not be done.

What first drew me to create the *Leaders in the Trenches* podcast was the opportunity to get to know some amazing people. It's been a huge thrill for me to read a book or see a speaker and then help them share their message with my audience. Plus, talking for more than 30 minutes each with leaders, authors, speakers, and the titans of business allows me to vicariously experience their journeys. I have asked probing questions to find out why they do what they do and what they had to learn the hard way.

I want to take this chapter and explore what some of my guests on the podcast have said about thinking bigger. Let's start with one key question that Dan Sullivan, founder of Strategic Coach, shared with me. Dan leads business owners to create self-managing companies. He and I hold many of the same ideas when it comes to personal growth. One of those commonalities is the belief in how mindset—the inner game—drives your actions and inactions.

He often asks clients and audiences this question:

*"If we were having this conversation three years from today, and you were looking back over those years, what has to happen in your life, personally and professionally, for you to feel happy with your progress?"*
—**Dan Sullivan**, Strategic Coach and Deep Thinker

Think for a second before firing off an answer. It has a future timeframe of three years. It covers both personal and professional aspects of life. This question is also about how you *feel* about your progress.

Can you answer this question? *Will you answer the question?*

Take a few minutes to ponder what would need to happen in your life for you to feel happy with your progress over the next three years.

I have answered this question for myself. I had a view of myself and my business at the time. I will honestly say that within two years of that day (yes, I wrote down my answers!) I had achieved 90% of everything on the list.

79

## THE TRAP OF SUCCESS

I was pleased for a moment. I reflected on my growth and impact with my clients. I smiled, and then I realized that I hadn't thought big enough. I lacked ambition and drive. I let my need for "How will I do it?" limit my future vision.

Has this ever happened to you when you attempted to dream big and achieve some scary goal?

I'm sharing this with you because I am now using the very same exercise again as I write this book. I am giving myself permission to dream bigger and not be hampered by what I think is possible.

Before we dive into how to think bigger and define your dreams, let me share with you what commonly gets in the way.

### The Impact of the "How Virus"

Have you lowered your expectations for a goal or a project because you got scared? If so, you're not alone. And it makes sense when you think about it. When you look into the future (even three years out), do you tend to look at what you want to create *and* think about how you will create it?

The "and" here is the key word. It is commonplace to limit your view of the future to fit inside the frame of reference created by the skills, talents, and experiences you have right now. You can stretch yourself somewhat, but you also limit your future by what you know today.

Every single time I have done this exercise, I have achieved nearly all that I could see for myself at the beginning. That's not good, because it means I played it too safe, didn't push myself beyond my existing limits. It's something I call the "How Virus." It's like a microorganism that stops you from thinking bigger. It's the thing inside you that must know *how* you will accomplish something before you let yourself dream big.

I'm going to give you seven simple principles to help you think bigger. Keep in mind, this isn't all you have to do. But based on hundreds of interviews with leaders in business, I know that this list will give you a great start toward thinking bigger in your personal and professional life.

Start with these seven principles, and keep building from there. Thinking big is a habit that we naturally grow and develop over time.

## Seven Principles of Thinking Bigger

### 1. Don't Make It About You

This is a big one. I start here because I want to remove the ego from thinking bigger. Life is about impact on other people. When you think about your journey over the next few years, who will you be impacting? Who will you be serving?

You don't have to start a charity to make this happen. It can be with your work. It can be with your money. It can be with your free time.

What do you want to do for those people?

Thinking bigger is easier when you focus on who you will be influencing with your work. This is a huge part of significance. When you clearly have others in mind, it is easier to overcome challenges that arise.

You can do this no matter what industry you are in. You can do it whether or not you are the owner of the business. You can make an impact on others. If you want to think bigger, get crystal clear on who you will serve and what you will help them with.

Another way to think about this is, for whom will you be a catalyst so that they can grow?

Don't forget your family. Or your employees or team members. Or your friends. Or even strangers who need your talents to achieve their next level of growth.

## THE TRAP OF SUCCESS

Without framing your thoughts in terms of other people, you're left with a flat and uninspiring list of goals that involve only you. You might get what you want, but likely it will come at a cost of the people who mean the most to you.

Think back to Sean Stephenson, who has his sights set on humanity as a whole in his drive to rid the world of insecurities. His goal is likely bigger than what I'd suggest you start with. Sean knows it is big, but that is what drives him.

> The thinking that got you here is also the trap—exactly the thing that will keep you from achieving next-level growth in your success and significance.

### 2. Remember That It's All about You

Yes, I know this runs counter to what I wrote above. I said to focus on others. But you also have to include yourself in the principles of thinking bigger.

When planning out your next steps in life, you are certainly going to want to grow your own thinking. Increase your standards, raise the bar, elevate what I call your MUST. Your MUST is what you will accept. And that starts with your *beliefs*.

The beliefs that you carry with you shape all of your results.

*"Whether you believe you can do a thing or not, you are right."*
—**Henry Ford**, Founder of Ford Motor Company and Father of the Assembly Line

Ford's quote is about your acceptance of a new future. This is a commonly used quote, but so powerful.

Besides believing in yourself, you must continuously push yourself to sharpen your thinking. If you like the conventional success you've achieved so far, then the thinking that got you to where you are right now has served you well enough. However, the thinking that got you here is also the trap—exactly the thing that will keep you from achieving next-level growth in your success and significance.

This means that you must continuously challenge the old beliefs. You must accept that what got you here can only deliver incremental growth for you going forward.

Thinking bigger is about finding new thoughts, then allowing those thoughts to transform the way you act. It works like this:

**Beliefs → Behaviors → Actions → Practices → Results**

Beliefs become behaviors. Behaviors cause actions. Actions, repeated over time, become practices. And your practices create your results.

My friend (and podcast guest) Shannon Graham uses this sequence to help his clients understand where they are in alignment with the internal beliefs and external actions in their lives.

Shannon has spent more than a decade helping high-achieving people think bigger and create the seemingly impossible. To follow his approach, it's important to have a clear understanding of the word "practices." What I mean by this is something similar to habits. A collection of actions over time becomes a practice. (I prefer to use the word "practice" instead of "habit" because of negative associations with bad habits like smoking that people want to break.)

Let's look at some practices that are getting in the way of you thinking bigger.

## Limiting Practices
These are five common practices that hinder thinking bigger. You may

relate to more than one, but in my experience one or two of these will probably shine brighter than the others for you. In fact, they may even seem like they are part of your "safety blanket" as you navigate through your days.

<u>Near-term thinking</u> — Focusing on the short term prevents you from seeing the long-term impact of your big ideas.

<u>Negative thinking</u> — Letting your inner critic keep you focused on doubt and fear prevents you from really thinking bigger.

<u>Perfectionism</u> — This disease is crushing, because it keeps you from taking real action, for example by accepting the excuse that you're "waiting for the right time."

<u>Productive Procrastination</u> — Putting off what's truly important will keep you from knowing what you can really accomplish. The "productive" part of this is making excuses that you are doing other tasks that need to get done; meanwhile, though, you know deep inside that you are avoiding what really needs to be done. For example, cleaning up your desk before you make that critically important call is a "productive" excuse. Cleaning your desk has benefits, but if you are avoiding the hard and uncomfortable tasks, your growth will be limited.

<u>Paralysis by Analysis</u> — Making something harder than it needs to be by over-analyzing the data and the possible strategies to pursue keeps you from moving forward.

Thinking bigger can't be done if you are not willing to challenge the old thoughts. This may sound simple, but it often requires you to talk it out with someone who can cut through your B.S. — a.k.a. your Belief System, which some will rightly call your bullshit. It is hard to do this for yourself because you get emotionally attached to your old ways. You have plenty of stories and excuses for why you think the way you do.

Even the best athletes in the world have coaches, and most have more than one coach. They are looking for the slightest edge for improvement. You don't have to break the bank to find a mentor or coach, but, in my experience, it is much easier to find someone who has been there before you and can help guide you to see what you can't see for yourself.

### 3. Create a Grand Vision and Mission

I believe vision and mission are essential parts of defining your future. The main reason for this is that a clear vision and mission pull you forward. They give you direction and allow you to really understand why you are doing what you are doing.

We will discuss this in detail in the next chapter, but for now: *mission* is knowing what's wrong with the world and how you intend to change it, while *vision* is what the world will look like once you've finished changing it.

Keep in mind that when I use the word "vision," it's more than just goals. It's a description of where you're taking your business and life, why that's important to you, and what the benefits will be of achieving the vision. It is typically a vivid view of the future.

I believe that every business and every person should have a vision. I also believe this vision should be something you communicate with your employees, partners, and clients. Yes, I'm specifically including your clients. When you tell them about your vision, they will better appreciate that you have a bigger perspective that has their best interest in mind. Vision could be the big long-term picture of what your company will be in the next three years, or it could be used to describe how you see the next project or initiative being completed.

Vision is centered on new results. To get to those new results, you have to avoid the trap that affects most people—the "How Virus" we discussed a few pages back. It's so easy to get caught up in questions like "*How* will I make this happen?" You have to avoid that, or else you'll spend your energy and time merely describing how to make the vision come true, instead of actually going out and doing it.

## THE TRAP OF SUCCESS

Creating your vision of a compelling future is so important that I've devoted the next chapter to it. Meanwhile, let's resume the seven principles for thinking bigger.

### 4. Manage Your Inner Critic

Your success is determined by your ability to manage your own thoughts and behaviors. That means there is only one person to blame when you fail. Oh, you may want to blame someone else, or something else. But the reality is, you can only look in the mirror for who to blame.

Let me ask you this: Why do we get in our own way?

Why do we let that inner voice stop us from what we really want? That voice shuts down your ability to choose the new and the bold. And that voice will criticize every change you want to make, even if you are not happy with where you are right now and *know* you need to make big changes.

I'll repeat what I said before—your inner critic is an **asshole**.

This might make you smile a bit, or it might just piss you off. Either way, if you are not content with where you are right now in life and business, you are likely listening to your inner critic. It will whisper anything it can to make you afraid to change. It knows how to stop you from making the leap. It will convince you to see obstacles in front of you as real, not realizing they are only in your mind. That's why I say your inner critic is an asshole.

Do you know what stands between you and what you really want? It's *you*.

If you don't have the life, the impact, or the money you want right now, it is your fault. You want to blame someone or something else for your challenges. You want to rationalize—find excuses—for why you don't already have it. So you make it about your current access to money, tools, people, or some other resource. Or you make it about the economy, or whatever you're lacking in your network or your education or your experience.

The harsh reality is that you're standing in your own way. One way or another, you're trapped in your comfort zone—because otherwise you would change it.

If you're ever tempted to make another excuse for not having what you want, think about Spencer West. Spencer lost his legs when he was five years old. That would stop many people, but not Spencer. He doesn't make excuses for his life or for not having legs; he finds a way to do what he wants.

 Your excuses are one of the primary roadblocks to your success.

For example, Spencer wanted to climb Mt. Kilimanjaro—all 19,341 feet of it. It took him seven days of crawling on his hands to reach the top. Think about how he dragged himself up the trail each day for hours and hours, inches at a time. Don't you think that was pretty hard to do? It didn't stop him. And if Spencer refuses to make excuses, you should, too.

Here it is again: *Your excuses are one of the primary roadblocks to your success.*

If that sentence triggers you in some way, if it makes you disagree or get angry, then it is especially meant for you. You might be thinking that I don't know your life and what you have been through. And you're right—I don't know. But I'm not wrong about what holds you back.

To think bigger or get something new in your life or business, you have to be willing to evolve out of your old ways. The solution—the new path you need—is inside you, if you will only let it out. But to stop getting in your own way, you have to stop letting your fears, your excuses, and your other old ways of thinking control you.

If you keep making excuses, you hand over your power to change to something or someone else. However, if you accept that you have no excuses, then you have the power.

My work as a coach has given me a unique perspective: I see so many people struggle in their lives and businesses, yet I've also seen some of my clients shift incredibly fast when they transform the way they think and behave. It's amazing to witness.

My hope is that you are willing to take this message in and use it. If you open yourself up to new thinking and muster the courage to apply the lessons of this book, you will see new ways of being and experience new joys.

Opening yourself up to that new reality requires managing your inner critic. I've formulated a series of five questions to help you do that. The first two are given below; I've also created a free tool that dives deep into all five of the questions, using insights from my own coaching work and more than a dozen inspiring leaders interviewed for my podcast.

*To access this tool for managing your inner critic, along with other free resources that complement this book, go to http://thetrapofsuccess.com/ companion-exercises.*

Here are the two questions to get you started on managing your inner critic:

<u>1) Are you willing to take 100 percent responsibility for your own success?</u>
This question aims to help you shift away from the practice of blaming others and toward taking personal responsibility for how you show up in this world.

<u>2) Do you let your fears control you?</u>
In Chapter 8, we talk about your fears, and this question aims at getting you to look at your fears from a new perspective.

Entrepreneurs and leaders—let me correct myself, *all people*—seem to encounter fears everywhere they turn. Fear is omnipresent.

I see the fears that come up and stop my clients. I see the fears they use to keep themselves from growing. I also see the fears that keep people from investing in their businesses. They have a fear of investing in themselves, because they don't trust themselves to do what it takes to make it pay off.

When you do what I do for as long as I have done it, it becomes easy to see the fears that keep people stuck.

### 5. Get Intensely Focused (and Deeper Is Better Than Wider)
You may think that "focus" is an overused term these days. We hear it on podcasts and we see it in books. My friend Joshua Seth recently wrote a book about it called *Finding Focus in a Busy World*. In it, he shares the secrets of tuning out distractions to get more done. Joshua shines a bright light onto how we subconsciously sabotage ourselves with distractions, and gives you dozens of ways to increase your focus.

It is so common today for people to juggle many projects at once. I'm guilty of this, too, and I've noticed that it is extremely difficult to get traction on the most important projects when you are constantly switching back and forth. Another friend of mine and guest on the podcast, Todd Herman, calls this "context switching" and has done the research to prove that we are losing precious moments as we juggle projects in our lives. Todd incorporates his insights from his work with Olympic athletes, corporate executives, and billionaires to help them perform at even higher levels.

Focus is a combination of art and science. You have to understand that the scattered approach is only costing you if you want to perform at a higher level. This becomes even more important as you expand your thinking. As you begin to think bigger, there is a common tendency to think about what *else* you can do. The common mistake at that point is to list out more things to do. But I invite you to think instead about focusing on going *deeper* with your work—working more intensely on fewer total things.

Think more deeply whenever you can. Amplify what is working. You will use your strengths as you focus on going deeper with your work.

### *6. Surround Yourself with Other Visionaries*

Thinking bigger by upgrading your network. In all seriousness, if all you changed was to hang out with other amazing people, that would improve your mindset and get you thinking bigger. You will find that those who have already reached a place of significance and exponential success in life and business have already embraced the other principles on this list.

So hang out with others who are doing something inspiring, with people who are doing "impossible" things. You'll be much more likely to be inspired to create something big in your own life.

Ask yourself: *Do I hang out with people who pull me forward or hold me back?*

Really think about your answer. Make sure you include the people you're closest to. It could be your family, your best friends, or your business associates. If they are thinking small, it will likely influence you to think small. And vice versa.

You've probably heard this quote before:

*"You are the average of the five people you spend the most time with."*
—**Jim Rohn**, Distinguished Author and Personal Development Legend

Rohn has been quoted millions of times for this short sentence. Why?

Because it's true. Sure, there are exceptions. Sure, you can point to one person who's able to act in isolation. But the norm is that it's very hard to break free of the thinking of people around you who are pulling you down.

Upgrading your network can include changing the live events you attend so you can find the speakers who inspire you. Or you could change your mentors, the mastermind group you belong to, or the communities you participate in.

The key here is that, no matter what it is, you have to engage with people at a deeper level. No more shallow conversations—you have to open up to what is really going on, for you and for them. You have to create trusting bonds that allow you to transform yourself and each other through conversations.

Let me ask you this: where do you think your limits come from? If you are hanging out with people who have crazy-awesome goals, some of that crazy-awesomeness will transfer to you. You'll begin to raise your standards and refuse to tolerate your old level of thinking.

I know the effect this has had on me. Over the past few years, I've regularly interviewed amazing people for my podcast. I have been masterminding with some of the greats. I have been coaching with the best performers in many fields. Many of these people are financially free; others are striving hard to create the impossible. And it has transformed the way I look at the world and at what I personally am capable of.

The bottom line is that you have to surround yourself with others who inspire you to think *bigger*.

### 7. Invest in Yourself
*Put your money where you mouth is...what you pay for, you pay attention to...put some skin in the game.*

## THE TRAP OF SUCCESS

Okay, you've likely heard this type of advice before. You know what the phrases mean, and when you have a business you love to work with people who understand the importance of that kind of investment. When others see the value in your services or your products, they are willing to pay you for it. This is common wisdom.

You're probably as thrilled as I am when a new client comes to your business. Even if you are not directly involved in sales, there is pride in seeing someone say "Yes" to making your business their guide for solving a problem or addressing some pain.

But there's also a breakdown—one that requires your utmost attention. I see so many people who spout business motivation and read books like the one in your hands, but then, when it comes to investing in themselves in a serious way, they stop. They let their fears take over. They don't trust that they will achieve the promised results. The don't take real action. In one way or another, they fail to realize that investing in themselves is really the best investment anyone can make.

If you're committed to thinking bigger, you need to shift your thinking about spending money on yourself, because you will need special guidance to achieve bigger goals.

It's so tempting to think "I can do it myself." But you must let go of that thinking.

I know this from personal experience. I love to do things myself— that's a big part of why I became an entrepreneur. But I also know the psychological value of writing a big uncomfortable check for my own personal development. I remember the knots in my stomach the first time I invested in an established coach. Writing those checks stretched me.

The results were outstanding. I starting landing new clients of my own, with amazing results, and expanding the whole way I did business. And here's the mind-bending part: it didn't even come from the coaching I received. The breakthrough in my business happened before I had my first session with my coach (who turned out to be fantastic), but after I had signed on and written that first check. Committing to a monthly payment scared me and pushed me to become a different person within my business.

Don't get me wrong, I'm not saying you have to work with *me*. You might be in an industry that I don't serve, or in a developmental stage that's not my sweet spot. You need to do whatever works for you. But if you want to grow, you will have to pull out your checkbook and declare a new future.

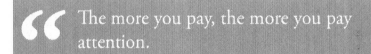

> " The more you pay, the more you pay attention.

The stuff you get for free or on the cheap doesn't have as much value to you. If you pay $20 per month for a gym membership, it's easy to skip going to the gym. If you pay $200 per month, you're much more likely to use it. And if you paid your trainer $200 per week, you will likely never miss a session, commit fully to every single exercise, and change your eating habits, too. The more you pay, the more you pay attention.

If you are trying to think bigger, you are going to be more committed when you are willing to make investments in yourself.

### Thinking Bigger en Route to Significance

Thinking bigger is a crucial part of the path to significance. There is no significance in playing small. You have to take action to find your fullest potential and live at that level.

My interaction with Sean Stephenson was a life-changing example of that for me. Sean may be small and may seem to have physical limitations, but he has a huge heart and works all-out to serve humanity.

## THE TRAP OF SUCCESS

As you focus on your own ability to think bigger, don't let your vision be infected with the "How Virus." You can think about the specifics of how you'll do it later—*after* you've set a clear vision, and after you start seeing yourself as the person who is ready to live out that vision.

As you work through the rest of the book, keep in mind *The Seven Principles of Thinking Bigger:*

**Don't Make It about You** — Have something bigger than you that compels you.

**It's All about You** — Realize that you have to change your being to receive your dreams.

**Create a Grand Vision and Mission** — Your vision and mission define where you are going and what it will look like when you get there.

**Manage Your Inner Critic** — Be wise enough to quieten the inner voice that says you are not good enough.

**Get Intensely Focused (and Deeper Is Better Than Wider)** — Practice deep focus to see what is truly possible in your life.

**Surround Yourself with Other Visionaries** — Find others to rub shoulders with who think bigger than you do; you will force yourself to grow along with them.

**Invest in Yourself** — Find areas of your life and business that deserve investments in training, mentoring, and coaching. It is okay if it scares you; do it anyway.

In the next chapter, we look at the essentials of clarifying your mission and crafting your vision.

### Questions to Inspire You

1. What's your biggest dream? What scares you?
2. What does extraordinary look like to you?
3. What has prevented you from living the life you have always wanted?
4. Which of the seven principles evoke the most resistance to your natural way? Why?

# CLARIFYING YOUR MISSION & CRAFTING YOUR VISION

If you are working on something exciting that you really care about, you don't have to be pushed. The vision pulls you.

**-Steve Jobs, Co-founder of Apple and Visionary Leader**

## THE TRAP OF SUCCESS

**"I believe we should go to the moon."** On May 25, 1961, President John F. Kennedy announced before a special joint session of Congress the dramatic and ambitious goal of sending an American safely to the moon before the end of the decade. He didn't mince words about how hard it would be:

*New objectives and new money cannot solve these problems. They could, in fact, aggravate them further—unless every scientist, every engineer, every serviceman, every technician, contractor, and civil servant gives his personal pledge that this nation will move forward, with the full speed of freedom, in the exciting adventure of space.*

You know the outcome. On July 20, 1969, Apollo 11 became the first human flight to land on the moon.

Going to the moon was a huge step for space exploration and for the United States. It started with a new idea of the future and activated not just one person, but literally thousands, to achieve something that most people believed impossible.

The vision that President Kennedy painted through his words gave Americans an emotional connection to a new destination, described the challenges to be met along the way, and articulated the new actions required to make that audacious dream a reality. It changed where we were headed as a nation.

A lot of ink has been spilled about clarifying your mission and vision, so you may encounter some things in this chapter that you've seen before. But your challenge—and mine—is to reframe our thinking, even in seemingly familiar areas, so we can escape the trap of success and achieve the breakthroughs required to attain new levels of success and significance. You have to inspire new thinking for yourself (and maybe your company) just like President Kennedy inspired new thinking for Americans.

The alternative, in my own experience and in working with many clients, is bleak. I've seen how damaging it is to a person's growth when they don't have a clear sense of mission or the clear vision of the future. So as you read this chapter, I urge you to join me in thinking through and shaping your own mission and vision in a new way.

### The Destination

Do you ever get in your car without having a destination in mind? Probably not often, right? So it makes sense that you would have a destination for your personal and professional life.

I don't know what proportion of the people I talk to in business that are operating without a clear understanding of their mission or a clear vision for the next three years of their work. But based on thousands of conversations on these topics, I'd guess it's something like four out of five.

Think about that: maybe 80 percent of the people I meet in business—and this includes a lot of "successful" people—can't answer the simple question "What do you want?"

In general, it is all too common for people to have no end goal, no end zone, and no final destination. Having a vision means having a clear idea of the future that guides you and your work (and your company).

### Not Just for Entrepreneurs

We all need a vision that tells us where we are going. This is not just for entrepreneurs. You could be an employee who wants to do something remarkable within your company. Or you may want to do something else beyond your current situation *someday*. I believe that having a vision for that now will help you prepare yourself for that day. I believe your vision is what shapes what you do and don't do now to get what you really want.

Even when you can appreciate the importance of vision, you are likely not putting enough soul into crafting a powerful vision that connects the emotions inside you to your future. If you are completely happy with what you have now, great. If you are not happy now, you have to be willing to change what you are doing and seeing in the world. You can't keep settling for similar goals over and over with hopes of achieving something bigger than what you have already done. Which reminds me of one of my favorite quotes:

*"Insanity is doing the same things over and over again and expecting different results."*
—**Albert Einstein**, Theoretical Physicist and Uber-Genius

Clarifying your vision will create new actions, and therefore new results. I want you to join me on the journey to creating a new vision. A vision that will allow you to achieve so much more—to create something so profound that you are drawn into the dance of success and significance.

It's important here to emphasize the distinction between mission and vision. Most people see these as similar or even the same. However, it is best to look at them separately.

## The Mission

Your mission is your North Star. It is the guiding light to what you are creating. It is your purpose. It is what fills you up. The drive to create significance within your work requires a mission that pulls you through the turbulent times. In fact, I believe you won't achieve significance if you have not clearly defined your mission.

You can't have a powerful mission without it being intertwined with your soul and your identity. These are big concepts that we're sometimes leery to address—but mission really is *that* big and important.

A proper mission spells out what's wrong with the world and how you intend to change it. Vision is what the world will look like once you've *finished* changing it.

# CLARIFYING YOUR MISSION & CRAFTING YOUR VISION

In the absence of a mission, you are only going through the motions each day, probably just to collect a paycheck. That may sound harsh, but if you are going through the motions I mean for it to be harsh. As long as you let yourself remain stuck in that old rut, you *cannot* achieve either significance or breakthrough success, much less both.

Later in this chapter, I'll show you how your vision and strategies will make your mission come alive. Your vision and strategies can and should be flexible. However, your mission is a simple description, mostly unchanging, of what you are here in this life to do. It is about more than just business, and much more than just making money.

Your mission is the driver for your vision. The mission is what you want to be known for. A proper mission spells out what's wrong with the world and how you intend to change it. Vision is what the world will look like once you've *finished* changing it.

Think back to President Kennedy's declaration about sending a man to the moon. During that period of the Cold War, the United States had fallen behind the Soviet Union in space exploration. We had advantages they didn't have, yet they had reached milestones like having an astronaut orbit the earth before we did. President Kennedy's mission became a way for us to "plant a flag" for the genius of the American people. (Pun intended.)

I would be guessing to say exactly why President Kennedy wanted to go to the moon, but as the leader of the United States he was driven to declare a future that challenged us with common goals and engaged our thoughts around something bold—something that would be impossible without nearly a decade of hard work and problem solving by countless people.

That is what I want for you. I want you to have a mission so scary that it activates you to think bigger and evolve into the person that you can be with courage and persistence.

In other words, mission is less about you and more about how you want to impact society, the world as a whole.

When you have a mission that is bigger than you, you see the world differently. You give yourself the ability to look beyond your personal needs and deliver on something much bigger.

Mission is to vision as the acorn is the oak tree.

### Unpacking Your Mission

A true mission changes the game in several ways:

- Mission gives you direction for your life and work.
- Mission connects your work to the impact you want to make in the world.
- Mission shares your core values with others.
- Mission fills your soul with joy when you are working it.

Mission is a huge part of the significance that you are striving for. When your mission is aligned with your work, you have a sense of purpose that you are not just existing in the world as it is, but *creating* the world as it should be.

I want to tackle a big misunderstanding I often encounter when I mention the need for a personal mission. A lot of people I talk to will emphasize that they have a family to provide for, which they take to mean that is their mission. However, I feel like they are not seeing mission through the lens of contribution to society. My belief is that your mission is something that your family will see and be inspired to be a part of, too.

Believe me, I understand the demands that come with supporting loved ones. I have a loving family, and I am here to provide for them. Yet the mission you undertake to achieve deep fulfillment, real significance, and breakthrough success is likely to go well beyond serving only your family. It is about your impact upon all of humanity.

# CLARIFYING YOUR MISSION & CRAFTING YOUR VISION

## My Mission Was Off

Let me tie this back to the failure of my first business—not just on the "2x4 day" when it all came crashing down, but in the years before that, when I was focused simply on making money.

From 2001 to 2010, I worked hard to build my company and increase my profits every year. I didn't have a clear mission for my life like I've just been describing to you. To the degree I thought about it at all, I reasoned that my mission was to provide for my family.

It's understandable. Even if you don't have a family—or just don't have one yet—you surely do have people close to you whose well-being is important to you. Of course you want to be there for them, and to meet your responsibilities.

Now, though, I see that significance goes well beyond family.

In building my sports tour business, I did provide for my family financially, and that felt good. However, I also felt empty inside whenever I pondered why I was not doing more for others. I had a view of my potential that was not being realized. I knew I could do more.

Looking back now, I see that whatever ill-defined mission I had for my life and business was really only about me. It's embarrassing to say, but I was simply selfish; that selfishness made me suffer, because I could not feel fulfilled so long as I was focused primarily on myself.

This brings me back to why I wrote this book. During the time I'm describing, I was trapped by my success. I want to help you see what I couldn't see then—that marching toward selfish, shallow goals could never bring me fulfillment like a real mission could.

Take a look at your goals. (You do have them written down, right?) How many of them are about *you*? How many are about what *you* want? How many are about what you want to *have*? Give yourself a few minutes to make this assessment now, and please be brutally honest with yourself about what you see.

## THE TRAP OF SUCCESS

If your goals are 95% about you, you are seeing life and work like I was in my first business. Looking back on that time, I realize that I didn't see anything wrong with my focus on making more money for the business and for my family. It felt noble. And I see that many other things in my life at that time were also all about me. I feel the old emptiness in my spirit as I write these words about my selfishness. Today, though, I see myself through a new lens, so much so that the old version of me seems like a stranger now.

When I think of mission now, it is drastically different. Today my professional work is helping others do what they think is impossible. I am charged up to start work each Monday, and I work hard all week to help people achieve their missions and realize their visions. This is fulfilling to me. This is my significance. This is my growth and contribution to society. I feel a swelling of joy inside me when I write this because it is what feeds my inner being.

It can't be emphasized often enough: A mission is not focused on you... it must be focused on others. Your mission clearly defines who you are serving and what you do for them, and it ought to be simple and inspiring.

Let's look at some individual examples:

*Gene Hammett — Serve leaders to go beyond what they believe is possible.*

My mission should resonate with what you read in this book about continuous growth, facing fears, having courage, and creating the dance of success and significance. The word "leader" to me means anyone that wants to make a change for the future. It could be an employee or an entrepreneur. It could also be a coach or a father. I want to activate others to live a life of contribution AND success.

*Sean Stephenson — Rid the world of insecurity.*

In case you missed Chapter 4, I want to remind you that this comes from a man who stands 36 inches tall due to a rare bone disorder that stunted his growth.

Here are some corporate examples:

*Google — Google's mission is to organize the world's information and make it universally accessible and useful.*

*NIKE — To bring inspiration and innovation to every athlete in the world. If you have a body, you are an athlete.*

*Patagonia — Build the best product, cause no unnecessary harm, use business to inspire, and implement solutions to the environmental crisis.*

*To get free companion exercises that will help you define your mission, along with other free tools that complement this book, go to http://thetrapofsuccess. com/companion-exercises.*

Remember, a powerful mission has clarity. Your mission has an emotional connection to YOU. It is soulful. It inspires you to create a different world than is visible today.

### From Mission to Vision

That new view of the future is your vision. A vision, quite simply, is a picture of what your success and significance will look like at a particular time in the future.

Vision grows out of mission, and then it serves as the foundation for everything that follows—your plan, your strategy, your tactics. Your vision can play out at many levels. It could be as grand as the entire five-year plan for your company; or it could apply to something intermediate like this year's marketing strategy; or it might be really granular, say in reference to a particular business opportunity. At any level, the point is the same: you need vision to gain clarity and confidence about the future you are creating.

You can develop a vision for just about anything. As an example, let's say you're about to have a specific conversation that you know might be tricky. Think about the desired outcome or result. How will you feel at the end of the conversation? Think about the other person's emotional state. Happy? Sad? Angry? Then work on how to create the desired result. What will you say? How will you say it? Where do you want to hold the conversation? What must happen to set up the conversation? You get the point.

"Crafting your vision" might sound grandiose, but in fact it's quite simple—it's exactly the process of analyzing and planning out the end result of whatever scenario you're facing.

By describing the destination or future, vision will create these benefits for you individually or for your company:

- Vision pulls you into action. (I use "pulls" on purpose. As the opening quote of this chapter expresses, Steve Jobs believed that a truly powerful vision pulls you to action.)
- Vision serves as a lens to focus your strategies, projects, plans, actions, and skill development.
- Vision can be critical to building a thriving business that encourages raving fans.
- Vision clarifies your role in the future of your organization. If you're an employee, you may be looking for more responsibility; if you're a business owner, you may be looking to change the nature of the business, or to have less day-to-day responsibility in running it so you are free to pursue bigger things.
- Vision sets your target.

Walt Disney is a good example of someone who had a grand vision. Disney's mission was to create a never-before-seen experience filled with magic and joy—one that would change entertainment beyond anything ever created by unlocking the imagination of children. As he transformed that mission into a vision, he pictured every aspect of his first theme park from beginning to end. People called him crazy, but Disney knew what he wanted to achieve to reach his goal of creating a magical kingdom. His creation ultimately became a landmark, not just on the physical map, but in the history of American business and culture.

### Enemies of Your Vision

We all face challenges in our personal and professional lives, and failure is a natural part of dealing with those challenges. It's the same when you are creating and implementing your vision, but don't worry: you can overcome any setbacks.

Let me share with you some of the "enemies" that will try to keep you from crafting your vision—things that will limit or block your progress. As you read the following list of **internal** enemies, think about how they could affect you, and how you could overcome them.

1. "I know what to do, I don't need a vision."
2. "The vision process takes too long, I am in a hurry."
3. "I already have a project plan [or business plan, strategy, blueprint, etc.]."
4. "It is impossible to know what my vision is...we are just getting started."
5. "It is too expensive to take the time for this."
6. "It will change down the road, so why do it now?"
7. "I lack the skills or resources to include [some important thing] in my vision."
8. "I need to be realistic because the thing I really want is too hard."
9. "I don't know how to do that, so it can't be part of my vision."
10. "My vision won't be ready until it is perfect."

Number 10 is especially important. A vision needs to be specific, but it will never be perfect. If you spend too much time crafting your vision, you will find it hard to take action when needed. A vision is critical to your success, but do not let yourself be paralyzed; drive ahead to make your vision real.

The **external** enemies to your vision can be the people who tell you to be "realistic" or to work on something "attainable." They are the people in your life who can't think big for themselves and have likely let their own dreams slip away. You may love those people, but don't listen to them. Later in this book, we will look deeper into how to surround yourself with people who will empower you to set and achieve a bigger vision.

### How I Used Mission and Vision in My Life

As you know by now, everything changed for me on January 15, 2010. The loss I suffered on that day made my career shift immediately. But it also caused my personal life to sink to a new low as it alarmed my wife, unsettled our family, and led to a devastating crisis of confidence for me personally.

Within a few weeks, I realized I needed to focus on my future. I didn't have any ideas or plans, but I did know that I wanted to work for myself again. I needed a mission and a vision for my future.

My mission would now have to be something bigger than me— something that could never be stolen or wiped out. I realized that basing my business on making money was something that could be lost again. I wanted a business based on helping other people and creating as much value to humanity as possible.

I can't remember what triggered me to think of the following quote, but it helped me through a tough time and helps me today in business and life relationships. I feel like this quote connected me to my mission— and that I am living it today.

*"People will forget what you said, people will forget what you did, but people will never forget how you made them feel."*
—**Maya Angelou,** Author and Activist to End Suffering

It is precisely this sentiment that made me realize the changes that needed to be made in my professional life.

## CLARIFYING YOUR MISSION & CRAFTING YOUR VISION

My new mission was to help leaders activate their full potential in business and life so that they could achieve both significance and exponential success. I strive to help them create businesses that make a difference in this world. I help to create renegades, rule-breakers, and champions. I also want them to have fulfillment during the journey of building their businesses.

I wanted to create a business that makes people feel good about themselves and improves their lives. That mission emotionally pulls me to do what I do.

My specific path was influenced by an experience years earlier, when I hired a business coach, Linda Finkle. During the early years of my sports tour business, I needed help to see what I could not see in the way I was running the company. The investment was minimal, just over a thousand dollars, but the impact was profound. It felt amazing to be heard and understood by an expert, and it gave me clarity on what to do next. With the coach's help, I turned my company into a multi-million dollar business.

Reflecting on this in the dark days after my business collapsed, I realized I wanted to be a business coach, but that my own coaching practice could be about something more than helping entrepreneurs simply make more money. My practice would combine my natural talents, my business skills, and my greatest passion—helping people better their lives.

After eighteen months of working for others and doing coaching on the side, I decided to fully commit to my mission and to creating my coaching business. It was 2012 when I started my company. In the beginning, I had trouble seeing the vision. I didn't really understand the business model and the challenges that go with it. I had a limited view of the future, with too many ideas and strategies competing for attention.

Finally, though, I decided I wanted to create a clear and compelling vision for the coaching business. It started with the people I wanted to impact over the next twelve months. I listed the number of clients I wanted to have and the kind of results they would get. I knew that if I focused on *their* results, the money would follow.

The clearest part to my vision was about writing this book and speaking on stages. I would lie in bed with my eyes closed and see myself holding up a book that the audience was eager to devour for themselves. When I think back on it now, I can see the background and even the faces in the audience. I can see them inspired to pursue a new future as I hold up my book. I didn't have the name of the book or any of the details about *how* I would get there. I just knew with certainty where I was going. I knew the destination.

Do you understand how my mission become the direction for my life? And how my vision then allowed me to see what I most wanted for the future?

When you decide on a new future with commitment and an emotional connection, your vision becomes clearer and more compelling. The vision begins to take shape the more you think about it, the more you think it is possible. My hope for you is that you will develop and put into action your own vision, just as I did.

### Share Your Vision

Once your vision starts to take shape, you can share your vision with everyone connected to it. By sharing the vision, I mean discussing it with colleagues, partners, clients, and employees. Get their feedback: determine which parts get the most attention, and which parts don't resonate. Some parts might not make the cut, but what is left will be strong and powerful.

A client of mine, Stefanie Diaz, followed this approach when she wanted to make a major change in her business. As we worked together over a period of months, she began to see the pivot she needed to make to achieve success and significance in her business. Stefanie started talking to friends and colleagues about her new vision for the business. The feedback was amazing, and she got some fantastic ideas just by sharing her vision. That simple act of sharing also gave her more confidence and support as she moved forward on making her vision a reality. Her experience confirmed what I've seen many times: sharing your vision makes it easier to reach the people who are attracted to your new picture of the future. They will *want* to be part of what you're doing. Your marketing will resonate at a deeper level, and the people who want to see your vision become reality will readily take actions that support your work.

In the months that followed that major shift, Stefanie altered nearly everything about her company. The business model, the pricing model, the audience she wanted to attract, the services she offered...they all changed. You won't be surprised to hear that her impact on the world—her significance—changed, too. All of that happened because she created a powerful vision and then shared it with the world.

When Stefanie changed her world, it allowed me in turn to take another step toward my own vision. In other words, *her* business taking off also contributed to *my* success and significance. The dance continues.

### From Mission to Vision to CHANGE

Having a vision is an important start to mapping out your future. It is important that your vision be incorporated into your company's culture if you own a business. Even if you don't own the company, you can still use your vision to guide yourself forward.

Integrating a vision into a company's culture may come naturally, especially if it clarifies and extends what the company is already doing. But if the vision implies a 180-degree change from the current culture, a more intentional approach will be required. So ask yourself, does the culture allow change easily? Are new and innovative ideas readily accepted? Whatever the case, if a company is experiencing high employee turnover, having a hard time attracting quality talent, or remaining stuck in a rut in the marketplace, it may be time for a new vision.

## THE TRAP OF SUCCESS

You will see that you can apply similar thinking to your personal vision. Do *you* readily accept innovative ideas and new behaviors? Are you stuck in a rut?

Creating and integrating a vision into an existing company culture can be accomplished in several ways, usually by the leader of the organization. Personally, I think a more holistic approach works best. All the major stakeholders or the leadership team need to give input into the creation and implementation of the new vision. This binds the organization together and presents a united front to the rest of the company.

*Check out a special lesson in the companion exercises that will walk you through writing down your vision. Go to http://thetrapofsuccess.com/ companion-exercises.*

### Review Process for Your Vision

Creating your vision is a journey that evolves over time. A vision is one of those living, breathing parts of a business that should adapt as you and your company grow. It isn't something you do once and then leave in place for decades, like creating a company logo.

However, be wary of revising the vision too often. How often you update it depends on how quickly your industry and your company are changing, but a common approach is to go through a quarterly review process for *small* adjustments and fine-tuning. In my opinion, you should **not** make your vision so near-term that it needs to be updated in a major way more than once per year. I'm using a 3-year term for my vision, but you can do what works for you. Just make sure you do it.

All that being said, make a point of looking over your vision each month to keep it firmly in your mind. Include your vision as a part of your company messaging. Looking at it regularly helps me stay focused, and when I need to make a big decision I think through how the options at hand fit with my vision.

# CLARIFYING YOUR MISSION & CRAFTING YOUR VISION

## Elements of a Powerful Vision

No two visions are the same. There isn't a simple form that you can fill out and call it done. However, there are some common traits. Your vision may not include all of the following elements, but it should convey most of them.

- States the future position of the company or yourself
- Describes the impact the company, or you personally, will make
- Offers some purpose for the work you do
- Describes who you will work with
- Lays out your values
- Conveys the emotions that go along with making the vision real

That last part is crucial. The point is to make your vision detailed and vivid enough that it becomes **real** to you. It stirs your soul and might even challenge your current identity. It makes you want to step into your full potential so you can create something of real significance. That, in turn, will pull you—just like Steve Jobs said—toward a new way of showing up in life and work.

## Length of Vision

You'll hear varying opinions about the proper length of a vision statement. Some people say it must be boiled down to a sentence or single statement, though I find that limits me too much. I prefer a vision that is less than one page, with some clear bullet points. Really, it is up to you. But whatever format you choose, your vision statement should be full enough to truly convey your future. At the same time, it needs to be so well-articulated and concise that someone who picked it up for the first time could immediately understand what it says and means.

Also, you don't really need to choose between longer and shorter versions, because the time you spend elaborating your thoughts in a longer version and then clarifying them in a shorter version will only deepen your thinking about where you are headed.

It is crucially—**crucially**—important that you get those words down in black and white on the page.

### Writing Down Your Vision

I've talked with hundreds of people about creating new visions for themselves. I firmly believe that, if you want to live proactively (as we'll discuss more in the next chapter), you don't wait for life to happen to you. As I've been explaining throughout this chapter, clarifying your vision in precise, compelling words helps you define the life you want for yourself and those around you, and thus work harder to change and grow so you can **be** the person who attains that life. Fundamentally, it's no different for you as a lone professional than it was for President Kennedy articulating the dream of going to the moon.

It is crucially—**crucially**—important that you get those words down in black and white on the page. Having it in your head isn't enough; it won't compel you. As you've been working through this chapter (and especially if you've gone through the companion exercises available on my website), you've probably been making notes about your vision. It's time to pull them into one place and flesh them out into a real vision statement.

Go back to the bullet points in the "Elements of a Powerful Vision" section above and think through each one again. Organize your thoughts in a way that makes sense to you, being sure to address most or all of those elements. Hash it out into a rough draft of your vision statement, and don't worry if you go well past one page; you want depth and clarity, and in your rough draft you might find it on page three.

When you've poured all of those thoughts into words on the page, ask yourself these questions:

• How clearly can you see the future for yourself?

- Is it still fuzzy?
- Is it incomplete?

Use your answers to revise your statement, over and over if you have to, until it fits on one page and truly conveys your vision. Keep that private version for yourself and make an appointment to review it monthly from here on.

Now you're ready to boil down your vision into a shorter version that you can easily share with prospects, clients, and partners. You will probably need to adapt the shorter version depending on who you're talking to and what you're talking about. Doing that, by the way, will again improve your thinking about your vision, because it will help you understand even better how it impacts different people or parts of your life. And, as in the example of Stefanie given above, it will inspire the different people in your life to help you achieve your vision.

To help you write your own concise vision statement, here are some examples:

**Gene Hammett** — My personal vision is to create a transformational coaching business to help visionary leaders to become THE choice in their market, not just A choice. I speak, write, and coach to inspire others to grow beyond what they believe is possible. My books guide millions to transform themselves. My speeches engage audiences to laugh, live, and matter.

**Alzheimer's Association** — Our vision is a world without Alzheimer's disease.

*(This is a great example of a short and sweet vision statement that also embodies the organization's mission.)*

**IKEA** — At IKEA, our vision is to create a better everyday life for the many people. Our business idea supports this vision by offering a wide range of well-designed, functional home furnishing products at prices so low that as many people as possible will be able to afford them. Our human resources idea supports this vision by giving down-to-earth, straight-forward people the possibility to grow, both as individuals and in their professional roles, so that together we are strongly committed to creating a better everyday life for ourselves and our customers.

*Again, I urge you to make the most of the free companion exercises available on my site to help you hone your vision. These include an audio training on vision creation and worksheets to guide you through the stages of developing your personal vision. Get it all at http://thetrapofsuccess. com/companion-exercises.*

A clearly expressed vision statement exists to guide you and those around you, whether the vision applies to you personally or the work of a whole company. You may even want to develop separate vision statements for yourself and your business, each of which will serve its own purpose in different settings.

In working with clients to help them shape vision statements, I have seen an unmistakable trend: whether the exercise is taken on the personal or the company level, those who put in the effort to develop a clear and compelling vision are far better prepared for the ups and downs of the journey required to achieve breakthrough success and significance.

## Using Your Vision

One of my clients, Derek Hart, founder of <u>GetTheGigs</u>, came to me a few years ago when he was unclear about what to do with his business. He had built a branding and creative agency that he was not thrilled about. In fact, he had come to dread the day-to-day operation of it.

In a vision-crafting exercise he did with me, Derek described why he started his business in the first place. Sure, he needed to make a living, but Derek knew that he had started his business for more than just a different way to earn a buck. Our conversation showed Derek that, before he could have what he wanted, he had to get clear on his mission and vision. Derek decided to rededicate himself to his business and work through that process with me.

Previously, Derek didn't have a mission or vision—he just showed up to work every day and shuffled through all the tasks, projects, and problems. Now, though, he has a clear mission and vision, which allows him to see where he is going and his overall purpose for building the business.

Derek's mission is to rid the world of mediocrity in branding and design. He has refined it over the years to focus on professional speakers, so that now his business helps speakers get more gigs by creating branding and design elements that quickly and powerfully position them as authorities for their particular markets.

Once Derek achieved real clarity about his vision, his revenues grew almost instantly. He was pulled toward his new future. And because he's so clear about where he's going and why, others have wanted to join the effort. That is what has allowed him to achieve significance with his work, along with exponentially greater success. Derek's vision continues to evolve as he has achieved his goals and is making a bigger impact on each new client he has. His work is getting better, and his confidence is rising with each new milestone he reaches.

If you're going to embrace your vision and make it real in the world, you have to change the way you interact with the world. In the next chapter, we look at the power of the reactive mode and how to break free from its grasp on you.

### Questions to Inspire You

1. What would your business accomplish if it had no restrictions?
2. What if you knew you could achieve *anything* you wanted?
3. What is your mission now?
4. What would your vision be if you thought bigger than ever before?

# BREAKING THE REACTIVE MODE

" A leadership culture is one where everyone thinks like an owner, a CEO, or a managing director. It's one where everyone is entrepreneurial and proactive.

-Robin S. Sharma, Leadership Speaker and Peak Performance Activator

## THE TRAP OF SUCCESS

Remembering back to running my sports tour business, this was the reality of starting a business and being new to leadership.

Every day was the same, and every day caused stress and anguish that I could not manage to break away from. I started the day with a plan: I had my list, it was prioritized with color coding, and there were spreadsheets to help manage the business. My intention was genuinely to focus on that list.

But once the team started showing up, they would mention issues that needed my attention. We would discover customers who had problems that only I could handle. Maybe I needed to buy something for the office. Whatever the specific reason, I would always get sucked into the day-to-day minutiae of the business. I didn't see it at the time because I was living it. I was more of a firefighter than a CEO.

The point is, I was reactive to the "fires" that showed up, and that was extremely stressful. It seemed to never end. I can feel my body tense up just remembering that time in my life. In one sense, I felt needed because only I could address these problems. But overall, the load was heavy on me as I attempted to grow the company.

Being a firefighter is not the way to run your company. You likely can relate to this in your own work. Spending all your time putting out the fires of the moment leaves you with no time for the projects that will grow your business beyond where you are. You could say that this is a different form of the trap of success. Without all those clients creating all those fires, I would not have had a business.

Back then, I operated in a blindness that seemed to never stop. I struggled daily until I broke free from that way of being. Finally my coach at the time was able to show me what was really going on. She asked me to step back and look at my business from a different perspective. In only a few months of coaching, she helped me double the profits of my small service-based business. In fact, the experience of working with my coach is one key reason why I am a coach today. She listened to me and gave me the space to become the real CEO of my company. I felt heard, and that gave me clarity about my next steps.

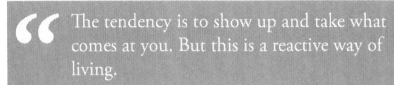

> The tendency is to show up and take what comes at you. But this is a reactive way of living.

Now let me help you the same way. Start with this question:

**What percentage of your day-to-day work is reactive versus proactive?**

The tendency is to show up and take what comes at you. But this is a reactive way of living.

For most people, the norm is to *react* to life. We jump at the buzzes, beeps, and bings. We respond to every call and email when it happens. We attend to the things that are important to everyone else.

But a reactive way of being limits your ability to create the life and business you want.

To create new results—significance and exponential success—you have to take purposeful action towards your life projects. Making that shift to being proactive in life is a game changer. The basis for creating the life and business you want is about defining and making it happen. You don't do that by being reactive to the world around you.

### Becoming Proactive
Making the decision to be proactive is easy. Applying the discipline is hard. Really hard. Again I promised to be brutally candid with you, and this shift is not easy if it has been ingrained in your life for years. You have to shift away from the old habits.

I've had many clients who have wanted to make this shift. With them, I use a model that I discovered in my coach training that has had tremendous success. I am certified as a coach through Newfield Network. The primary foundation of their program is Ontological Coaching, which consists of knowing how you are "being" in the world. This concept is extremely powerful in many ways. One of them is that it allows you to step back and look at how you are showing up versus how you want to show up. It uses three domains to look at your "being": Body, Emotion, and Language.

In general, the BEL (Body-Emotion-Language) framework is a model for observing your way of being and can be applied to anything. One way I use this is to get others to break from their normal patterns of conversation around their lives. A key part of my coaching is applying the BEL framework to being reactive versus proactive.

*The companion materials on my website include a worksheet to help you through this analysis for yourself; the worksheet gives you typical answers that come up when high-achieving people discuss reactive and proactive modes. To download it, go to http://thetrapofsuccess.com/companion-exercises.*

| MODE | PROACTIVE | REACTIVE |
|---|---|---|
| Body | | |
| Emotion | | |
| Language | | |

I have worked with hundreds of people using this framework with many areas of focus that allows them to answer questions like:

**BODY:**
- How would you describe your body when you are in **reactive** mode?
- How would you describe your body when you are in **proactive** mode?

## EMOTION:

- How would you describe your emotions when you are in **reactive** mode?
- How would you describe your emotions when you are in **proactive** mode?

## LANGUAGE:

- How would you describe your language when you are in **reactive** mode?
- How would you describe your language when you are in **proactive** mode?

Then I ask a final question: **What does filling in this chart tell you about yourself?**

I invite you to play along here so you can begin to open up these insights for yourself. You won't find the real power of this exercise without actually writing down your answers.

### Using the BEL Framework

I remember one of my clients—we'll call him Robert—who came to me with a desire to get more done. Robert wanted to make more money and take on more responsibility. We talked about his typical day. He was quite proud of how well he could work under pressure. He said he could get more done in the last two hours of the day than most people can do in a whole day.

I asked, "What happens after that?"

Robert said, "I'm exhausted. I just want to go home and collapse."

It was quite obvious that he was reactive most of the day, and then would shift his energy to a higher gear toward the end of the day to get everything done. That pattern meant that he rarely had time to do what he wanted to do, and rarely had time to do the most essential things.

## THE TRAP OF SUCCESS

Robert and I talked about the impact of working this way. He was confident that he "worked well under pressure." I have heard this many times before. Heck, I have said it about myself before. We kept talking about the stress it caused him at work, in his professional and personal relationships, and even in his home life.

I offered Robert a chance to better understand what was really going on. He accepted what I had to say because he was ready for a change. He decided that before noon each day he would complete all his other tasks and leave the afternoon open for meeting with clients. He also gave himself a longer lunch break, and even occasionally left some time for golf. Robert realized that none of that was possible without an overhaul of his work patterns.

I took Robert through the BEL framework so that he could see for himself his way of being. The questions were odd to him, and I didn't allow him to make excuses or justifications about the way he was acting.

After he filled in the framework with a few words or phrases in each box based on me asking the questions above, I asked him the final question: "What does filling this out tell you?"

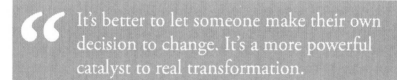

> It's better to let someone make their own decision to change. It's a more powerful catalyst to real transformation.

Robert squinted a bit and pondered the words on the page. He took it all in. Then he responded: "If I show up like this [pointing at the reactive mode column], I will never get what I want. And if I show up like this [pointing at the proactive mode column], I can get anything I want."

I smiled. This was yet another proof from my work that it's better to let someone make their own decision to change. It's a more powerful catalyst to real transformation. If instead I had taken a consultative approach, told Robert the value of being more proactive, and given him some training on how to do it, the process might have been interesting, but it would not have been transformational.

Robert had to figure this out for himself—like we all do. Using the BEL framework allowed him to see the way forward for himself.

You have to figure it out for yourself, too. Reading this might be interesting and eye-opening, but transformation can only come from the inside, not from the outside. In other words, *knowing* is not enough. You have to see yourself from a new perspective.

Once you decide to show up proactively, you will want to take action to continue your progress.

### The Proactive Mindset

Thinking ahead of the present and planning for the future is a big part of creating significance. In fact, I will be so bold as to say that without this mindset you will never have what you really want.

Waking up daily with proactive strategies allows you to create your vision of the future, but letting the reactive mode rule the day will drive you away from your future.

When you decide to operate proactively, you will encounter challenges that seem insurmountable—challenges like too many projects going on at once and too many goals that keep your attention switching back and forth. These are all common during the initial shift to being proactive.

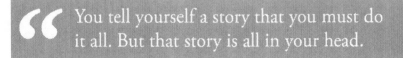

> You tell yourself a story that you must do it all. But that story is all in your head.

The initial shift to being proactive comes with immediate successes and relief. But then you notice that unexpected things crop up that need your attention. Trust me when I say that I understand this never-ending push and pull of clients, projects, and goals. You look at what you are doing with your proactive approach and wonder how you can get the new stuff done, too. You rationalize that you can do it all. This is also known as backsliding. Be careful here, because you're falling back into old patterns. You tell yourself a story that you must do it all. But that story is all in your head. It's just your inner critic telling you that change is not going to happen, even if the change is good for you.

In my experience, the shift to being proactive starts with a decision—the decision to cut off the constant scrambling and switching-back-and-forth. The decision that you have to make is not to be taken lightly. If it is, you will quickly slide right back into your old patterns.

You must make a commitment that does not waver. (We'll talk more about those when we discuss Larry Winget's approach in Chapter 10, "Playing to Win"). Commitments are not always convenient or comfortable. In fact, they will often be tested over and over. Your job is to make a deep commitment to become proactive.

I have seen that growth only happens through action. It may sound obvious, but you have to take action on being proactive. Intention is important, but falls short when you don't put it into action.

At first, you will be overjoyed with the areas in your life where you can be proactive. When you have lived a life of "reaction" for so long, it can seem like that's "just the way it is." But once you dive into being proactive, you will find a slew of areas in your life and work that you have neglected.

And once you start being proactive, you *will* see immediate growth. It will feel good—really *good*. You'll be planning and getting things done. You'll put systems in place to help you. If you are fortunate enough to have a team to support you, you will also need to involve your team in this new way of being.

Once you head down this path, the energy drain of being reactive will start to fade away. In some ways, proactivity empowers you because you are more in control—no more firefighting. Yet in other ways, you will feel guilt for what is not getting done, the fires that aren't getting put out.

It takes time for being proactive to bear fruit. I warn you about that now because the journey to get there is so worth it. You will create more value with your work and feel a sense of significance as you and your team get in sync. You'll be thinking days ahead, sometimes weeks.

But you may also start to feel exhausted, and that might make you feel like it no longer serves you to be proactive. That's when you need to take a step back to look at what is really going on. We so commonly miss this critical realization that I have a huge smile on my face as I think about how many times I've run into it even during my own transformation to being proactive.

### You Can't Do It All

It's that simple: You can't do it all. You can't just take all the aspects of your life and business in which you've been reactive for so many years and expect to change it all at once.

For that reason, I suggest that you start small with proactivity. Start by choosing one aspect of your life or business—something that's easy to manage—and be proactive on that one thing. It doesn't matter which one you choose; the key is just to pick one. It could be urgent. It could be important. But the real power comes from picking just one thing.

Break it down into steps. Decide the sequence of those steps. Look at what typically gets in the way of being proactive in that area. Remove whatever is unnecessary. Develop a new strategy for handling that one area. You can work with your team to create systems that work for everyone involved. You can then repeat the process for the next area of your life, but don't worry about the second area until you nail down the necessary changes for the first one.

125

## Putting My Podcast on Autopilot

I'll give you an example from my own work. My first area for being proactive in my coaching business was my podcast, *Leaders in the Trenches*. I love interviewing people and even just talking with prospective guests about being on the show. I *don't* love the other aspects of podcasting, and over time that caused me a lot of stress and struggle when it came to the weekly task of creating the show.

Honestly, the production of a weekly podcast isn't overly complex. In fact, it's laughably simple for me now that I have created 280+ episodes and continue to produce one each week. But it wasn't something I could laugh off back when I was in reactive mode.

I wanted to put a proactive system in place that made podcasting easy and fun. I wanted to remove the extra parts that I hated or merely tolerated and leave myself with just the parts I like the most. That meant building a team. I had to get intentional about the whole process so I could become proactive about it.

Because I started with this one area, I didn't get overwhelmed. While I have continued to refine my system, I can now say that I have recorded two months in advance for my podcast—and I keep that buffer intact, which takes away all of my stress about it. I have a team of people who support me with the aspects I don't like. Doing that has brought back a new joy to this part of my life.

## Building Your Own Culture of Transformation

Making the decision to be proactive will help you on your path to significance and exponential success. To get transformative results, you must take a transformative approach, and breaking free of the reactive mode is essential for that, no matter what kind of work you do or what your version of significance looks like.

I chose the Robin Sharma quote at the beginning of this chapter not just because it had the word "proactive" in it, but mainly because it was about culture. I have seen reactive cultures in operation, and it's true that they can work for periods of time. But time and time again I've seen that it's proactive environments that really drive a company and its employee to do significant work. A reactive culture is what happens when leadership does not make being proactive a priority.

The BEL framework is just different enough to get you to shift your natural way of showing up. It is something that you can use to make more informed decisions. It will guide you to look at your body, emotion, and language and thereby make your own shift from reactive to proactive.

Remember, the strategy of becoming proactive is best implemented one small step at a time. I say this from experience. I want you to make this transformation in your own life, and the most effective way to do that is to designate one area of your life or business that you will make proactive to give yourself the space you need for other areas of future development.

In the next chapter, I will explore the need for comfort and how it plays a vital role in where you are now. I will also share with you the virtues of leaning into your discomfort in a way that allows you to grow.

## Questions to Inspire You

1. What part of your day-to-day work makes you feel like a firefighter?
2. What impact has being reactive had on your work and your personal life?
3. Did you download and apply the BEL framework to your reactive and proactive work? What did you discover when you went through the exercise?
4. What is the first area that you want to make proactive in your life? Why?

# GETTING UNCOMFORTABLE

When God wants you to grow, he makes you uncomfortable.

-Unknown

## THE TRAP OF SUCCESS

I got a call from my friend Jason Swenk about his website. Jason is an experienced business owner, and quite a genius at marketing, who had recently sold his digital agency.

When he called me, he was obviously frustrated: "Do people sign up for stuff on your website?"

"Sure," I said, "I get about 30 to 40 people per month with no advertising." This was in the fall of 2013, before I began my podcast and before I started speaking on bigger stages.

After 18 months of having a website and blogging regularly, Jason was starting to get more traffic, but his frustration was that no one was signing up for his newsletter.

I went over to his site and clicked on a few blog posts. I liked his titles on the articles, but I noticed that they were all quite generic. I switched into coaching mode and asked him a question about his website and his writing. "Your writing looks good. I like the titles. But who are you writing to?"

He quickly said, "Small business owners."

> **No matter how good your skills are, or how broadly your services could apply, your job is not to attempt to serve everyone.**

I knew immediately that his answer was too broad. Aiming for a broad market is a typical response for any entrepreneur who is struggling to get more leads—whose marketing reality is not equal to their revenue expectations. I get it; I've heard it a thousand times before from clients and friends, and I have lived it, too. Essentially, no matter how good your skills are, or how broadly your services *could* apply, your job is not to attempt to serve everyone.

"Small business is not a target market," I told him. "It is something people say that really means they will do business with anyone who will do business with them."

Jason was silent. This is rare for him; he almost always has a response. We talked about his goals, and what he wanted to do with the "business." I use quotes here to be kind, as he didn't really have a proper business yet. Remember, he had been blogging for 18 months, but had no money to show for it.

Jason asked me, "What do I do about it?"

The conversation circled back to his audience. The ideal person to read his blog articles was unclear. Given the fact he didn't have any clients, I asked him, "Who do you have the experience and talent to help? Where would you add the most value?"

Jason again was silent. Then he blurted out, "I ran a digital agency for 12 years, took it to multiple millions in revenue, and sold it. I can help others do that too?" The inflection in his voice at the end of the sentence showed that he was a bit unsure of this.

I responded quickly with, "Why didn't you think of this before?"

Jason said, "I didn't want to limit myself."

*There it was*—the fear that comes up so often when I talk to my clients about their businesses. It's a fear that lives inside them that keeps them from establishing a real focus for their business. But focusing your attention and activity on a clear audience is the primary strategy that will get you the highest value from your work.

I asked Jason, "Why?"

He said the magic words, "It was uncomfortable to limit my business. I don't want to leave anyone out."

## THE TRAP OF SUCCESS

That was the core issue: Jason was running his "business" based on an emotional drive to be comfortable. Because of his desire to be comfortable, he didn't have subscribers, and he took 18 months to reach out to someone to help him with it. Well, to be more precise, he did tell me that he had seven email subscribers for his newsletter, if you counted his mom.

The moment he saw this for himself was the moment he could make the crucial decision: either keep doing what he was doing, or get uncomfortable. The decision for Jason was obvious. He was ready to make a change. He wanted to go beyond where he was.

You likely have areas in your life right now that are comfortable—so comfortable they don't require you to make any changes. This story about Jason is a clear example of how seeking this comfort can keep you stuck in doing the wrong thing.

Later in the book, I'll come back to talk about Jason's next steps on his journey to building a highly successful expert business, which took place over the next three years. I'll share the major moments of his journey so you can follow a similar roadmap if that is what you want to create.

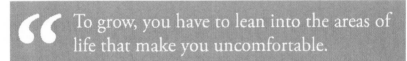

> To grow, you have to lean into the areas of life that make you uncomfortable.

First, though, let's talk about the desire to be comfortable and the need to get uncomfortable. All innovation happens when we step outside our comfort zone. To grow, you have to lean into the areas of life that make you uncomfortable.

Wait! When you read that, do you play the reel in your mind that you've heard all you need to hear about "getting outside your comfort zone"? It's old advice, and it's easy to gloss over it. But I want you to stop for a second and answer some questions for yourself: are you *applying* what you know? Are you doing it *consistently*? Are you feeling the unease of stepping outside your comfort zone *daily* and moving forward with courage anyway?

Seriously, take a minute to get honest with yourself about these questions. If you really are doing all of these things already, great. Even if you are, though, I believe that anyone can go still deeper by using what's contained in this chapter.

## Being Comfortable

There are times when comfort is the right way to go. Comfortable shoes are a gift when you're walking 28 blocks of Manhattan touring the city, for example. The desire to be comfortable is natural. It's safe and it feels good. Seriously, who would choose to be uncomfortable in the everyday activities of life?

But let's look at one example of a daily activity that many of us pursue in which we choose to be uncomfortable: exercise.

Do you go to the gym to be comfortable? Do you go for a six-mile run to be comfortable? Do you go to yoga simply to go through the motions and be comfortable?

I guess some of you might seek comfort, but for most of us going to the gym is about pushing ourselves to a new level. Lift more weight. Run or walk a bit longer, or a bit faster. Hold that yoga pose deeper and steadier than before.

Now, if you are rehabilitating yourself from an injury, then you might be seeking comfort. That's okay. But I also know that if you are injured and using the workout to get back to your new normal, resting at home would be more comfortable than going to the gym—yet you're getting in there and doing the work anyway.

We work out not to be comfortable, but to get *uncomfortable* by pushing ourselves more than we have in the past. That's where we transcend our old boundaries, grow, and improve.

133

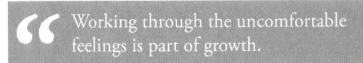

> Working through the uncomfortable
> feelings is part of growth.

### Comfort Is the Enemy

"Enemy." Think about that word. An enemy is one who opposes you in a contest or struggle.

If you feel completely safe in your work, you are not in the right area. You want to always be going a little further than where you feel safe.

Until we purge ourselves of it, we all have a negative inner monologue that whispers to us when we are doing something new or reaching further than ever before. That is **fear** talking. When you listen to that voice, you have a choice. You can let it stop you, or you can take it as an indication that the thing being feared is important.

When you look for places to get uncomfortable in your business, you find new opportunities. When you feel that twinge of discomfort, you are just about at the right place to do something exciting.

Being the CEO or founder of a business, or being a leader in your current role, is a constant series of growth opportunities. You will always be facing new areas that will cause you to feel uncomfortable.

We put a positive spin on them when we call them "growth opportunities" or "chances to learn," but the fact is that professional and personal growth means falling on your face and getting back up, again and again. And that comes with a measure of pain.

If you're reading this book, you likely have already experienced hundreds or thousands of those moments when you had to grow as a person to handle the situation in front of you.

As I shared earlier, my first few years as the CEO of my sports tour business were filled with more moments when I felt like I was a "firefighter" rather than a CEO. I consistently showed up to the office each day to handle the next problem: client problems, cash flow problems, employee problems, tech problems.

In those moments, it makes sense to want more comfort in your life. It gets tiring being responsible for so much, with everyone looking to you for answers. Really, it's no wonder that, once you turn the corner that allows you to be comfortable in your business, you just want to stay in that zone.

### Getting Uncomfortable

The first time I heard "Get comfortable with being uncomfortable," it came from my mentor David Neagle. It took me off guard, because I had thought that my role as an entrepreneur was to build a business of freedom and create a life of comfort.

Yet I leaned into David's message about being uncomfortable, because that was the place for growth.

It caused me to rethink what I wanted from my life and business. I began to notice the times when I was uncomfortable and felt the resistance. I pondered the moments that scared me.

I wanted to lean into them to see what would happen, and it worked. I called more people and invited them into meaningful conversations about my business. I started speaking at more conferences. In short, I started to see the benefits of being uncomfortable.

Working through the uncomfortable feelings is part of growth. Transforming the pains of the day-to-day—all of those "learning opportunities"—into real moments of growth is an absolutely necessary skill.

This is about training your brain to seek the edges of your comfort zone and then step over that line. You keep doing that enough, and soon you'll begin to seek that rush of not knowing what is on the other side, pushing beyond the comfort that once seemed normal.

Getting comfortable with being uncomfortable is a must-have if you want to join the dance of significance and exponential success.

### Over Time, Discomfort Becomes Natural

Here's an analogy for you. From my perspective, learning to play golf is possibly the most frustrating thing a person can do. If you have ever tried to swing a club, you know what I'm talking about. Starting out, you have to be concerned with trying to coordinate a hundred different parts of your body—your head, your hands, your hips, your wrists— just so you can swing the club effectively. None of it feels natural to begin with; in fact, it challenges the way that your body naturally wants to work. And while you're learning a proper swing, you're *also* not hitting the ball worth a damn, which is emotionally frustrating. It is just an uncomfortable experience.

But you have to push through that discomfort to see results. Somewhere in there, you swing the club with proper form and rhythm, the ball flies straight and true down the fairway, and it all feels easy. Over time, the motion starts to feel more natural, and your shots start getting longer, more accurate, and more consistent. You enter a virtuous cycle of improvement as you get your reps in and deepen your experience. And then your golf coach tweaks something else, and something else, and something else, and you find that your thirst to play better keeps you going through each new round of discomfort.

Business works the same way. You have to train yourself in new habits, and that will keep on happening as your business continues to grow— and as you continue to grow. Seeking comfort at every stage of growth is not going to prepare you for your next level. I have never seen a business that runs extremely well by avoiding discomfort.

Setting and achieving big goals requires you to get uncomfortable. Speaking on big stages—physically or metaphorically—requires you to get uncomfortable. Going after a bigger client or offering something new requires you to get uncomfortable. Leaving a crappy job that does not inspire you is definitely going to be uncomfortable.

If you want significance and exponential success, there isn't any other way. Your decision to seek out discomfort when you set your goals, formulate your strategies, and do the work day in and day out is what will keep you growing as a person and as a leader. It is what will keep your company growing, too.

## The Need for Comfort Will Kill Your Dreams

Your growth is up to you. No one is going to save you, and no one is going to hold your feet to the fire day after day to make sure you're staying comfortable with discomfort. You have to do that for yourself. It is your own responsibility, and uncomfortable growth is a necessary part of the process.

To grow, you have to come to regard being uncomfortable as the only way you can evolve. It will make you feel uneasy. It may cause resistance—within yourself and those around you who are threatened by change. It will likely cause fear.

But the need for comfort in everything you do will keep you from what you really want in life.

*If* you let it. You have to commit yourself to not letting that happen. Seth's quote below is one way to see risk and comfort.

*"Begin to realize that the safest thing you can do feels risky and the riskiest thing you can do is play it safe."*
—**Seth Godin**, Author and Prolific Blogger

In the next chapter, we look at the role of fear in your life, and how you must embrace it and overcome it so you can keep getting uncomfortable, and keep pursuing significance and exponential success.

# THE TRAP OF SUCCESS

## Questions to Inspire You

1. When's the last time you stepped out of your comfort zone and took on a new challenge?
2. How have you let the desire for comfort stop you?
3. What is your normal response to being uncomfortable in moments of growth?
4. What is one time in your life where you felt uncomfortable but did it anyway and ended up achieving something new?

# LEANING INTO FEAR

Fear is the path to the dark side. Fear leads to anger. Anger leads to hate. Hate leads to suffering.

-Yoda, Jedi Knight and 26-Inch-Tall Guru

## THE TRAP OF SUCCESS

I let fear stop me. I let fear keep me from want I really wanted.

When I think back about my first business, I feel pain down in my soul even saying that I let fear keep me from creating something innovative and groundbreaking. I let the fear stop me, even though I wanted it so badly that it consumed me.

Maybe you don't understand this—or maybe you've been there, too. Fear is abundant in our world.

As I mentioned before, I realized what I was up against when my wife got tired of me talking about it. She finally asked me, "What are you going to do about it?" That halted me in my tracks. I knew something was going on inside myself that had been stopping me. I realized that I had been stuck in a zone of pre-planning or pre-commitment for years.

What was holding me back?

Well, it was me. Specifically, it was my fear of losing what I had built already—a classic case of being trapped by success. I also had a desire to do something more purposeful and fulfilling. After my son was born in 2007, I was horrified that he would follow in my footsteps into the sports tour industry. I didn't even want him to know what I did for a living. I wasn't ashamed of what I did—I just wanted more for him.

Hindsight is 20/20. I can look back now and see all of this clearly.

I had made decisions based on practicality and comfort, growing my company incrementally using the same strategies that had made me successful before. I kept going with the same approach, and it worked. I made more money and still had my free time. And I never went after that deeper achievement that I longed for.

### What About Your Fear?
Is fear stopping you? If it were, would you admit it?

I know that when I used to encounter these questions, my first response was always something other than acknowledging fear—a justification or an excuse. I would always have something else to blame.

Fear is a sneaky thing. It is invisible. It lurks inside us with patience. It knows exactly what will get to us and cause us to question that next step or project or strategy. Your fear has an intimate knowledge of you and will do anything to get you to pay attention.

Yes, there is also such a thing as genuine, valid fear. That noise in the middle of night will scare you—and it should. Genuine fear is there as a survival mechanism to keep you safe. And it affects us so infrequently that we often don't know exactly what to do. Do I grab a bat? Do I put on pants? (Yes, putting on pants is a good idea. Just in case.)

You know there has to be a big "but" here, right?

Ready? BUT...most of the fears you experience are created in your mind. They are not valid. You create them to *feel* safe, but they are not in fact needed for your survival. You make up stories that support your beliefs. And that type of fear is irrational.

Let me share a method that will tell you if a fear is rational or irrational.

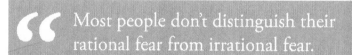

> Most people don't distinguish their rational fear from irrational fear.

**Rational fear** usually involves the potential of physical harm (that bump in the night might be an intruder with a gun). This type of fear exists to protect you from real threats, or from doing something stupid like jumping off a cliff.

**Irrational fear** usually involves the potential for embarrassment or loss of something, as in the fear of making a sales call or speaking on stage. This type of fear exists to keep you from changing and growing.

## THE TRAP OF SUCCESS

The problem is that they feel similar, so most people don't distinguish their rational fear from irrational fear.

There is another huge difference between rational and irrational fears. Rational fears don't stop you from taking action. Think of the bump in the night—you really *did* hear something. You processed it, and then you got up to find the source of the noise.

Contrast that to irrational fears, which tend to stop you cold. We tend to make them bigger than they really are and build stories around them—which creates an excuse to stop doing whatever it is that's triggering the fear.

In other words, you find reasons to play it safe.

Fear will never go away completely in our lives. But would you be willing to look at fear from a new perspective? Could you humor me a bit and get really curious about fear?

What if fear is a sign? What if the fear is here to tell you something other than STOP or WATCH OUT? What if fear is actually a signal to grow?

That nervous energy and resistance to change is your inner voice saying, "Hey, watch out here. This is important." You can interpret it as a message to *lean into* the fears so you can realize your greatest potential.

Remember that the biggest fears arise when you are faced with the biggest opportunities.

### The Types of Fears

You must face fears in your journey to achieving and becoming more. Period. No one—and I mean no one with sanity—is immune to fear. You are not alone in your fear. I know it can feel lonely as you are building something meaningful and unique in the world. That feeling of being alone is persistent.

But if you are striving to reach a new level, or looking to achieve a goal, then fear is something you will inevitably feel within yourself. Those who are successful distinguish themselves from the rest because, instead of trying to avoid fear, they put it to work. They use it to build a sense of inner courage, and as a signal to pay closer attention.

The types of fears that you will face may vary depending on your own experience and view of life. Yet I group most fears into one of the four different types explained in the pages that follow.

As we go through the fears, I will explore each one, then give you a way to deeply understand all of them with an internal and an external approach. This will help you move forward. This will show you how to lean into fear, if you choose.

But let's get one thing straight: *avoiding fear does not work*. Avoiding or ignoring fear will either prevent you from making a decision to grow, or it will put you in real danger of loss.

### The Fear of Failure

This fear seems to be everywhere in business, and even shows up in personal issues.

The fear of failure surfaces as "It won't work" or "It won't work for me." Those might seem like similar statements, but in fact they are quite different.

"It won't work" is about your belief that the strategy is flawed or that the approach is not the right one. "It won't work" is not a personal issue, though it is still a story that you tell yourself that's rooted in the way you see the world.

"It won't work for me" is about *you*. It is about your current skills and talents. It is about the way you see yourself when you believe your situation is different or you aren't competent enough. It really is about this inner feeling of not BEING enough.

143

## THE TRAP OF SUCCESS

Either way, the fear of failure stops you. In fact, it's the number one roadblock that keeps people from even starting. You say to yourself, "If I don't try, I will never fail."

Have you ever said those words? Be honest. Have you thought them?

Your particular way to express this fear might be to say, "What if it doesn't work out?" or "What if I lose money on this?"

Or maybe you just put off starting, telling yourself the lie that you'll get to it "tomorrow" or "someday." One of the biggest symptoms of fear is procrastination. You put off doing the thing that would stretch you because of fear.

The fear of failure shows up when you don't take risks. You stay in the comfort zone. You don't make a decision. You maintain the status quo. And you have a host of excuses ready for anyone who challenges you about it.

### The Fear of Success

This fear is about who you will become when you achieve this big goal or have _____ in your life. The fear of success, in other words, is about the difference between who you are now and the future person or life that you think will come with the achievement. Fearing the changes that success might bring (social life, family life, personal life, work stress, money, etc.) is an important part of that.

This fear is not as common as the fear of failure. However, in hundreds of conversations with business owners and people, it does come up. These are the types of uncertainties they admit to when they tell me why they are not taking action.

I remember an accomplished doctor sharing her fear of success with me. Let's call her Susan. She saw me speak on a stage in front of 600 entrepreneurs about creating exponential success and the way that kind of success dances with significance. After the talk she tracked me down.

She started telling me about a big idea she had. You could tell she was excited. Susan wanted to tell me about the real problem that her patients faced and about how the stuff currently on the market did not address the real issues—and most of it didn't work at all. She told me about her years of experience with the issue, and the new approach she had developed because of all her experience and talent.

I was thinking, "She is onto something." I was also thinking about the confidence she expressed about actually solving the problem. And I thought how easy it would be to make this a great business for a board-certified doctor with decades of experience.

I asked Susan a few questions about the business and the idea. Then one question changed the conversation. I asked Susan, "What is stopping you from making this happen?"

She paused and looked down at the ground. In a soft voice she said, "I'm afraid of what will happen with my personal life if this is big."

She was excited about something that has real value in the world and meets a real need. And she knew she was the one to provide a unique solution to this important problem. Yet what held her back was the fear of success.

I had to dive into this with more questions. I was curious. Susan explained that she enjoyed her private life now, especially her life with her kids. She was afraid of the fans who would come into her life because of the amazing product she had conceived.

This is the clearest example of the fear of success that I can give you. It happens to a good number of people, and it stops them from achieving their dreams.

## The Fear of Change
This fear is pervasive, but simple to explain. Change is a huge issue for many people. Being able to face the fear of change requires changing your mindset.

# THE TRAP OF SUCCESS

You see change as either pain or progress. In my experience, it always comes back to one of these.

When you see change as pain, you will fear it. You see the downside of any new way of doing things that you encounter. You see all the reasons why it won't work. You see all the reasons—the excuses—why you should delay. The fear of change is powerful.

Those who see change as progress don't worry about the new personal and financial realities they will have to face. They embrace the newness and even meet change with a sense of joy about figuring out how to cope with it.

## The Fear of What Others Will Think of You

This is the granddaddy of the previous fears. It really is the mega-fear. Or do you prefer the master fear?

The fear of what others will think of you involves your relationships with the people around you and their ideas of you.

**Failure** — If you fail, you get scared about what family or friends—or even rivals—will say or think about you. You focus on the possible negative repercussions of doing something different, and your thoughts navigate to the disappointment or rejection that it could draw from others in your life.

**Success** — If you succeed, you get scared of what everyone will say about you once you have money or become a big shot. Think about how calling someone a "big shot" is an old-school way to cut down the person who has confidence and success. You may fear the way the relationships in your life will change along these lines.

**Change** — If you change, you get scared of how others will see you. You wonder if they will think that you "sold out" or gave up your integrity, for example.

The fear of what others will think of you is what comes after the initial fear, and it is what piles on top of your other insecurities.

Living in any kind of fear is debilitating. But understanding those fears by addressing them and understanding them can invigorate you. It will empower you to face more fears.

## Avoiding Your Fears

One of the most common struggles we go through is procrastination. Procrastination is often a response to fear.

Remember "productive procrastination," the limiting belief I introduced in Chapter 4? It is a concept that means completing tasks that may be valuable in themselves, but are being used to avoid other, more important, tasks that we fear tackling. It's a classic type of avoidance, and it can especially affect "successful" people: you avoid dealing with your fears by keeping up the appearance—even to yourself—of doing "productive" work. But deep down you know you're not doing the *real* work.

That's just one out of many mechanisms of avoidance, and the types of things we avoid—well, that's an even longer list. To help you think more about the fears you avoid, here is a partial list of fears that show up frequently in professional growth. Which can you identify with?

1. The fear of making sales calls—of asking for business.
2. The fear of following up with people you already know. This means giving up too easily when people say no or don't return your call. (Fact: Did you know that 60 percent of sales are made after the fifth attempt?)
3. The fear of raising your prices, which reflects that you don't feel valuable enough to ask for the price you really want or deserve.
4. The fear of not being enough—which keeps you from letting your brilliance shine.
5. The fear of speaking in public—which keeps you from sharing your message with your ideal prospects.

6. The fear of letting go of things on your to-do list.
7. The fear of delegating because someone can't do it like you do. This is an expression of your need to control.
8. The fear of the niche, which is rooted in a scarcity mindset, not abundance. It's related to the fear of missing out—and taking whatever you can get. (This is what Jason Swenk experienced in the last chapter.)
9. The fear of investing in your business, which is often reflected in underspending on events or marketing.
10. The fear of investing in yourself through training, events, coaching, and consultants.

*"Do the thing you fear the most and the death of fear is certain."*
—**Mark Twain,** Legendary Author and Charmer with Words

If you want to achieve significance and higher levels of success, you must confront your fear.

But before you can even confront it, you have to acknowledge that it's there in the first place. It can be daunting, and you'd be surprised at the lengths people will go to as they try to run away from it.

### Understanding Your Fears Deeply
Let's dive into these fears so you can be prepared for your journey toward greater success and significance. No matter how unpleasant, all fears serve a purpose. And the best way to find that purpose is through an understanding of those fears.

How can you put your fears to use so you can continuously create better versions of yourself? Rather than avoiding your fears, you can channel them for your professional growth.

Think of the fear of failure. Too many people think that trying and failing is the worst that can happen. In fact, though, the highest-achieving people know that failure is an intrinsic, absolutely unavoidable, step on the road to success. In fact, you should be concerned if you're not failing *enough*—because it means you're not trying and risking enough.

That realization allows us to look at failure quite differently:

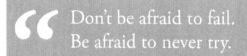

> Don't be afraid to fail.
> Be afraid to never try.

I love this approach to failure. I love it so much that I look for places in life and business that trigger fear so I can analyze the importance of that task or strategy. If it's triggering fear, it might be something really promising—something that takes me out of my comfort zone to a new level of success. That's how I use fear in a positive way. It is what allows me to grow.

Complacency with your current life may sound like a Zen thing, but I don't buy it. You may not dream as big as I do. That's okay.

But avoiding fear is not a recipe to a happy life. Avoiding it only hurts you and inhibits growth. I think the truly Zen thing to do is to have gratitude for where you are and who you are, and try to see things in the world as they really are. (Remember the difference between your truth and *the* truth?) And then you challenge yourself to continually grow.

I have had many conversations with clients, podcast guests, and others who have learned to face their fears. In the next few pages, I'll give you two perspectives that allow you to deeply understand the nature of your fears—the internal approach and the external approach.

The better you understand your fears, the more likely you will be to muster the courage to use those fears as a spur to further action. This is about working *with* your fears. I am not going to tell you to grow a pair and just do it. That approach can work sometimes, but here I'm giving you a way to let your fears be a signal to keep growing, while also avoiding excessive risk. Trust me on this—I'm the guy who lost it all to get here and write this book. Use the fears that come up to help you keep risks in check.

Keep in mind that this works for the small projects or the big ones. Either way, it will help you get clear on what the fear is and thereby help you navigate forward.

Let me share with you the internal and external approach to understanding your fears.

### The Internal Approach

Don't accept that your feelings of fear are shallow. Don't accept that there is not more to learn.

I have seen tremendous results by working with clients on fear using the internal approach. Nearly every time I ask these questions with my clients, it's in a live conversation, which means that I can insist that they don't hide or avoid the questions. They are compelled to address them. It works because they actively want to move forward with their fears by understanding the deep sources of them.

One way to make this really work for you is to have someone you trust help you with it. It can be a business partner or an accountability partner. It can be a mentor. It can be a friend. Whatever the case, it should be someone who wants to support your growth and not someone who impedes the changes you are facing or considering.

You can do it alone, but for better results, get someone to help you. Business is not a solo sport, and neither is life.

I call this the "Fear Discovery Exercise." It is a deep dive into the fears that come from doing something new or changing direction. As you work through it, there are a couple of things to keep in mind. First, this is not about fixing your fears. It is about understanding them. They don't need to be fixed. Second, don't let yourself stay shallow here; go deeper than ever before for best results. Go beyond the normal.

Here are the four basic questions in the Fear Discovery Exercise. The explanation of each question is below.

*You can also download a free worksheet and video for the fear discovery exercise from* http://thetrapofsuccess.com/companion-exercises.

1. What are your fears? List them one by one.
2. Why are they here? Describe *why* each of these is a fear.
3. How can you understand this fear better?
4. What are you going to do with your new awareness of these fears?

### What are your fears? List them one by one.

Make a list of your fears, and be as specific as possible. If you aren't doing this with someone, ask yourself and pause. Take 60 seconds to let the question sink in. Stay with the moment, and the discomfort. Then, start writing. I would suggest that you do this with pen and paper. Typing is great, but the old-school scribing by hand has a deeper connection to your neural pathways. Give yourself a full 10 minutes on this one to ensure that you get to the real fears.

Organize your thoughts into a list of the fears. Can you combine any of the fears into a mega-fear? It is best to avoid overlap and go with the fears that seem to really nail what you are experiencing. You can have more than one fear, and likely you will.

This is your chance to name the fears. Choose a common name that allows you to make clearer decisions moving forward.

### Why are they here? Describe WHY each of these is a fear.

This is your chance to dive into the reasons why each fear shows up for you. I want to highlight that you will do this for each fear on your list. If you listed three, then you will do this exercise three times. GO!

"Why" is a powerful word. Keep writing. Keep going to get it all out. And when you think you are done, add on the question " And what else?" (This is the "AWE" question that I share with you from my podcast interview with Michael Bungay Stanier who wrote the wildly popular *The Coaching Habit*.)

Again, this works better with someone who will help you get clear about it. You can keep asking "And what else?" until you have exhausted all the thoughts swirling around in your head. The deep aspects of this come in the follow-up questions, so don't stop.

Here are a few complementary questions to sharpen your understanding of these fears:

- What is the true source of this fear?
- Where has this fear shown up before?
- Why does it keep showing up?
- Why do you avoid it?
- Who are you afraid to disappoint or hurt?

When you're done, pause. Organize your thoughts. Write the real "why" for each fear you have on your list.

### How can you understand this fear better?

Use this question to go deeper for each of the fears. Beyond the naming of the fear and finding the source of the fear (the "why"), here you can list out anything that arises in your mind about addressing each fear. Remember, this is not about *fixing* the fear. It is about understanding the roots of your fears so you can find strategies to address them. Ultimately, it helps you reduce risks as you use the fear to propel yourself forward.

Don't jump ahead. Brainstorm it. Ask yourself, "and what else?" here too.

Organize your list again. Get ready for the final question of this exercise. But first there's one more concept to introduce.

## Understanding Your Fears Is the Path to Risk Mitigation

The feelings of resistance that cause indecision are commonplace. You have looked at your fears from new perspectives that now allow you to create a better plan. Use the fear to your advantage. Don't let it stop you.

Let your fear help you clarify the risks of the moment. The fears that come up are signals pointing to growth as well as a protective mechanism to prevent loss. Realizing that you have these fears for good reasons can raise your spirits; the fears themselves will guide you to create strategies that allow you to manage whatever the risks are that caused the fears to arise in the first place.

My clients are constantly pushing new boundaries and brushing up against their fears. We talk about what really is causing each fear to see what message it provides. For example, it might indicate that they need more preparation time, or need to find more support in that area. The lesson here is to listen to the "message" that comes from fear so that you can create a way to reduce the associated risk. This is how fear can lead directly to risk mitigation.

## What are you going to do with your new awareness of these fears?

Here you can list your actions from the previous work for each fear. This is where you get clear about the next steps.

You may decide, in some cases, that the fears are false or weak. It's a false fear if you realize that you really aren't afraid of moving forward—you just didn't have a plan or strategy. Doing this exercise has exposed the need for a plan, so now you can move forward. Weak fears are ones that cause doubt and uncertainly, but don't actually diminish your resolve.

Finally, you may decide that some or all of the fears are reasonable. Now you have a series of next steps that allow you to better understand the fears that keep you from going forward.

153

## THE TRAP OF SUCCESS

The internal exercise for understanding your fears is powerful—if you do the work. I have used this simple exercise for myself and with clients. In fact, some clients have credited this one approach as a way to break the grip of fears that had long been keeping them from growing and doing something significant.

Now let's look at your fears from another angle. This exercise helps you understand your fears through external analysis. In the simplest terms, it is looking for clues from those who have taken this journey before.

### The External Approach

There is tremendous value in taking a big goal to an expert or someone who is a few steps beyond where you are right now. For example, I am a coach, a speaker, and a writer. In every new endeavor I undertake, I reach out to someone who has walked a similar path. That's one reason I have a podcast—so I can interview amazing people who have done incredible things.

The results for me have been fantastic. In every case, I have been better off by talking through my ideas with someone else. My fears have washed away or faded with just one conversation, or sometimes a few conversations for bigger moves.

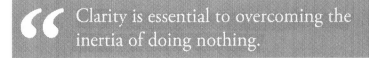

> Clarity is essential to overcoming the inertia of doing nothing.

I know this approach seems simple, and many people will say they have already done it. But I encourage you not to skip this part if you still aren't sure about your next steps. Clarity is essential to overcoming the inertia of doing nothing.

Talking to an expert is one of the easiest things you can do to deeply understand your fears. I have talked to a dozen people about writing a book, and it only gave me more clarity for actually doing it. The book in your hands is proof that their advice worked.

For one episode of my *Leaders in the Trenches* podcast, I interviewed Pat Flynn. Pat is the founder of *Smart Passive Income Podcast*. He has built a 7-figure expert business. Specifically, he talks about the online world and creating passive income.

If you want to listen to that podcast, it was episode #134: "On the Other Side of Fear is Amazing." Check it out; you will definitely appreciate the depth of his approach. http://leadersinthetrenches. com/134 will take you there.

During the interview, Pat talked about building an elite team of people to support his business. He also shared his journey of overcoming fear in all parts of the business.

Pat talked about:
• Starting his business after being laid off
• Creating videos
• Starting a podcast
• Speaking on stage
• Hiring his team members

Each of these transitions in his business caused some sort of fear. He was open and vulnerable about what he went through that keep him stuck. He also shared that the fears were just signals of a growth opportunity. We discussed his own hesitation and resistance, and also shared that, each time he had the courage to overcome the fears, it was an amazing experience. The results catapulted his business to a new level. That's why I named the episode "On the Other Side of Fear is Amazing."

When Pat sees new opportunities come his way, he looks for that fear. He takes it as a signal for imminent growth. His mindset about fear has changed as he has overcome anxiety and doubt to create amazing results.

*"When something scares the heck of me it makes me think I should do that."*
—**Pat Flynn**, Captivating Speaker and *Smart Passive Income* Podcaster

## THE TRAP OF SUCCESS

Pat shared his specific approach with me, including how he now seeks out experts who are doing what he wants to do before he does it. Here are some of the specific questions he uses:

- Is it normal to feel like this?
- What is the worst thing that can happen?
- What are some tips that you have for me?
- What books should I read?

You can ask any questions you want. When you find the right person to help you, you'll see the power of this approach for minimizing your fears and helping you create strategies to keep going.

Pat uses the external method to overcome fear. Sometimes it's hard to do a thing—especially a difficult new thing—on your own. Asking people who have been down that road before you is a great way to deeply understand the fears that swirl around and keep you from going for your dreams.

### The Value of Understanding Your Fears

Fear can prepare you for your journey. It can alert you about where to research and plan. It can inspire and confirm your strategy. It can save you money by giving you the best strategies to minimize your risk or show you the right sequence of steps to take.

Remember, your fears are still there. Don't avoid or ignore them. *Use* them to propel you forward.

Implement the internal and external approaches to go beyond the surface level of the fears so you can fully understand your fears and give each of them a name. Use what you learn from the exercises to come up with your next steps. Over time, your mindset towards fear will expand. You will be able to shift your perspective about what fear is and what it means.

Today, I choose to let my fears be a signal to growth. I look at them with curiosity. I want to understand them. I want to get to their real source.

I want to be courageous. This is the way I choose to live instead of being controlled by fear—as I used to be when I ran my first business. Understanding your fears from internal and external angles allows you to move forward with courage.

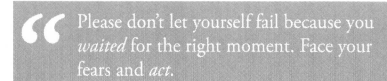

> Please don't let yourself fail because you *waited* for the right moment. Face your fears and *act.*

When you have courage, you can lean into the fear. Safety is seductive, but playing it safe is not the path to growth.

Please don't let yourself fail because you *waited* for the right moment. Face your fears and *act.* Doing that is essential to the dance of significance and success.

In the next chapter, we will explore courage—facing the fears in front of you.

**Questions to Inspire You**

1. Do your fears control you?
2. Have you taken the time to really understand your fears?
3. Do you have the courage to move forward anyway?

# BEING COURAGEOUS

"

It takes courage to choose hope over fear. To say that we can build something and make it better than it has ever been before.

**-Mark Zuckerberg, Founder of Facebook and Connector of More Than One Billion People**

## THE TRAP OF SUCCESS

Courage is often overlooked in our journey of life.

Over the years, I have had the honor to work with hundreds of people to better understand their personal growth. Most of that work has been with founders of companies and leaders inside companies. These are the people who gravitate to my work as a coach. I have been fortunate to witness the change inside people who move from living in fear to living with courage.

I don't take this fact lightly; in fact, it's part of my significance in this world. I firmly believe that God allowed me to be successful and also showed me the pain and stress of losing it all just so I can help others today. I believe that I have been through these things so I can better serve humanity. That's my journey in life.

In my work, I have seen many people stop themselves because of fear and doubt. I have seen them remain trapped inside of stories they tell themselves like "What might happen if it doesn't work out"? and "I just can't do that."

I have noticed that if you let fear control you, it will. If you let your fear stop you, you come up with the most excellent reasons for why you should wait or what else you need to achieve before taking action.

### "I Can't. I Don't Have a Website Yet."

One example here is the "website excuse." I have talked to so many people who are just starting out or maybe even have a little bit of experience. They want to speak at a conference or get their first clients. They are convinced they need a website before they do anything else. They argue and get all determined that this is their next step—when, in fact, having a website is not all that important. I call bullshit: you don't need a website before you can start getting clients or booking events.

The website excuse gives them a reason, which feels fully justified, to focus first on something they don't have any fear about. The reality is that most of those who focus on getting a website before they get started are scared to approach people and have real conversations. To be clear, a website *can* help you once you're certain of what you want to say with it and how you want to position yourself. But at the very beginning, not having a site is just an excuse for not moving forward.

And then I have seen people who have made the decision to not let their fears stop them.

Those people have courage. It takes a lot of courage to break free from what they have always done to create something new, or even something that others would say is impossible.

### Jason's Journey of Courage

I've had a few clients who have so much courage that they never even realized how important it is. For instance, I was having a conversation with Jason Swenk (mentioned in Chapter 7) about the book you're reading.

Jason and I were chatting about the premise of this book. He connected deeply with the idea of significance because he himself had felt the uneasiness of enjoying financial success without having the sense that his work mattered. Then I said that the concept also includes "how to break free from your comfort zone and find the courage to create significance."

He fired back at me, "I don't think courage plays a role in business. Courage is what our soldiers do on the battlefield."

I was shocked to hear him say so, and I went into a little rant about how important courage is for entrepreneurship and leadership. He paused for a second and said, "I have never seen it that way."

What happened after those two statements from Jason is where the magic happens. I asked him what was stopping his clients from making more money, other than the strategies and systems they were missing. Jason said that they were afraid.

161

## THE TRAP OF SUCCESS

I asked him, "What does it take for someone to stop being afraid?"

In a thoughtful way, he responded with one word: "Courage."

I realized that one thing that separated Jason from others is that, at least much of the time, he didn't have to think about courage. He is one of those rare individuals who does not let fear stop him. For the most part, he has courage flowing through his veins, to the point that it has become invisible to him.

However, even Jason faces the occasional crisis of courage. In a separate conversation, I remember Jason needed to make a pivot in his business. He had some fears, and we clarified them through a few questions. Then he shifted in the middle of our chat to, "...but I have to do this anyway." I'm smiling as I remember seeing him sit taller in his chair as he said that. He was no longer focused on why he couldn't do it, but on why he must make this big change.

Now, I know the outcome of that one conversation over lunch. It was a breakthrough for him. He discovered the courage to move forward despite his fears. Jason does not wallow in doubt like many people do. (Myself included: in the past I have also set up camp with my insecurities from time to time.) Jason talks through his doubts with me and makes a decision to let courage lead the way.

From that point in the conversation, he and I created a strategy that would address his fears. Then he took action instead of remaining stuck. And he got the results that he wanted. His decision led to a new revenue stream for his business.

Had Jason stopped because of fear, he would never have found this new strategy.

As discussed earlier in the book, shortly after Jason sold his digital agency, he started blogging in support of his next business idea. But his blog was broad and didn't create a compelling reason for anyone to engage in a conversation with him. I worked with him to help him get hyper-focused on his audience, and then to clarify his first offer for them. In our more recent sessions, Jason and I have discussed pivotal moments in the growth of his company. Jason gets all the credit—he did the work. I am just a catalyst for his growth.

Once he got on the right track, Jason ramped up quickly to a six-figure business. Within a year and a half, he was knocking on the door of seven figures. Plus, he has expanded the reach and effectiveness of his speaking, all while creating the lifestyle business he wanted. The real joy for me has come in watching him grow, transform himself, and find real significance with the work he's doing. Which, again, increases my *own* feelings of significance.

Jason is what I would call a "force of nature" in business. He sees what he wants and makes quick decisions. Jason's life and business now are where they are because he has the courage to make it so. Jason's journey to significance is one that inspires me to keep doing what I am doing. And for this, I thank him for being part of my journey to rebuild my life.

### Courage Precedes Significance

When you understand your fears and can make a commitment to move forward anyway, that is COURAGE. And courage is something that you cannot live without if you want to continue to grow and expand. Courage is a necessary part of creating a life of significance.

*"Challenging the status quo is the willingness to say what others are thinking, but don't have the courage to speak up and say."*
—**Srinivas Rao,** Founder of The Unmistakable Creative and Surfer

Srinivas (Srini) Rao recently published his second book, *Unmistakable: Why Only Is Better Than Best*. In my podcast interview with Srini, we talked about being unmistakable in business. He related it to making art so distinctive that your work does not require a signature—art so infused with your heart and mind that no one else could have created it.

## THE TRAP OF SUCCESS

At the core of his message is the ability to be courageous. Srini shared with me the importance of courage in his own journey from MBA to entrepreneur. He has acknowledged and dealt with his fears throughout life to find his current significance in the work he is doing.

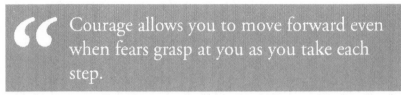

> Courage allows you to move forward even when fears grasp at you as you take each step.

When you have courage, you take action despite the fears and doubts that fester inside you. Courage allows you to move forward even when fears grasp at you as you take each step. In the absence of courage you will not challenge yourself to move forward and grow like you're capable of.

To use courage, you need to understand it. It's time to get insanely curious about courage, just as we did about fears in the previous chapter.

I want to show you how I have begun to understand courage in my life and my work by simplifying it into two categories.

### Two Types of Courage

In my life's journey, I have been fascinated with people who have created something big and are doing what many would think is impossible. This is one reason why I love the Olympics so much. The sacrifice and hard work to become the best has always fascinated me, especially when people triumph despite overwhelming odds against them. I love to talk with people whose goals are "insane" and scary to most of the world.

This is one of the factors that attracts me to my clients who are up to something meaningful. They are certain they want it, yet don't know how to make it happen. When I get to know them, I see patterns in how they operate and how they see the world. One of the key patterns

I've seen is what I refer to as the two types of courage—the type that comes in pivotal moments, and the type that's displayed day by day.

### Pivotal Moment Courage

When life falls apart and you fall on your face, you have a choice. You always have a choice. Let me call it out for you in the simplest terms:

1. You can let it keep you down, or
2. You can get back up again.

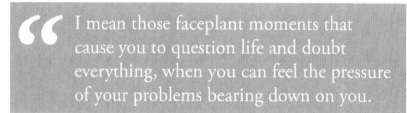

> I mean those faceplant moments that cause you to question life and doubt everything, when you can feel the pressure of your problems bearing down on you.

That's it. If you want to stay down, you don't need courage—and you wouldn't be reading this book. People who let their failures keep them down often see themselves as victims. They blame others and always have an excuse for why life doesn't go their way. They've stopped trying.

However, if you are the kind of person who gets back up, then you know that getting back up means dealing with fears. That process has to include admitting the lessons you must learn. Getting back up is a choice that requires courage.

In those pivotal moments, you have to pick up the pieces. You face the demons of doubt.

To be clear, I'm not talking about one of life's little stumbles. I mean those faceplant moments that cause you to question life and doubt everything, when you can feel the pressure of your problems bearing down on you. Those are the moments when you have to muster the will to fight your way out, calling forth every ounce of courage you have from deep inside you.

## THE TRAP OF SUCCESS

My own largest pivotal moment is clear to you by now. I lost millions of dollars on January 15th, 2010. In fact, losing more than $3 million in a 24-hour period is the kind of thing that most people might not recover from. Over the years I have shared my story thousands of times with friends and strangers. I've had some interesting responses, ranging from "How did you get back up and keep going?" to "Do you want me help you 'take care of' that guy?" (I'm surprised by how many people felt my pain to the point that they seemed willing to commit a heinous crime on my behalf. You have to laugh about it. Right?)

While those events were still unfolding, it wasn't completely clear that I was going to lose the money and have to start over, although the signs pointed that way. On the day after my discovery, I had been thinking nonstop about the possible outcomes. My wife, Amanda, had been thinking about the same thing. As we were talking about it, she said, "You are done with the ticket business." I could see the pain in her face. She had that serious tone that meant "This is not negotiable."

I had been thinking about it, too, and I agreed. I would not be going back into the ticket business. I had wanted out anyway, and had been thinking about what might come next for me. I told Amanda, "I don't want to be in tickets anymore. But I do know I will start another business."

I remember the strength she displayed going through the whole ordeal with me. She said many times that we would look back on the experience and see it as a *gift*. That was a wise perspective to take, though also tough to maintain while life as we knew it changed drastically, we had no money coming in, and the attorneys' fees piled up.

Those pivotal moments have a colossal impact on us. Mine made me change from the inside out. It was not just about closing down one business to start another. It was about completely changing my beliefs.

I had to find Pivotal Moment Courage so I could rebuild my life and my professional career. I had to fight to breathe at times. It was my rock bottom.

Yet the courage to get back on my feet was absolute. I had many fears, and tons of doubt. I had setbacks that caused me to stumble on the path. But courage remained constant, and I learned what resilience really was.

You may not have lost it all before, but you have no doubt faced other difficulties—those pivotal moments that have made you start over in some area of life or business. You've faced the doubts. You didn't know how you would overcome your challenges, but you held out hope that you would. And you took action, despite the fears.

This kind of courage along the journey is easy to see, and it's an important part of creating a new future. However, it is not the complete picture. In those big moments, we may change and fight for new results. But those reactive changes don't give a complete view of the courage needed to transcend conventional success and enjoy the dance between significance and exponential success.

Here's the second type of courage:

## Everyday Courage

The pivotal moments stand out, but probably 99 percent of your life is ordinary. This means that most of your days are filled with getting your projects done and working with others—and that our everyday struggle with fear and doubt actually shapes more of our future than the pivotal moments do.

When we show up every day and just do what we do, we tend to fall into ruts that become invisible over time. We do what we've always done, and find comfort in acting and performing exactly the same way over and over.

It's what I call the Drift. It means just showing up and letting life carry you down the river. The Drift has a mild current and steadily propels you, not necessarily in a direction you have consciously chosen. The Drift is not good for you, but you think it is because it feels normal. It feels comfortable, which is the problem we looked at in Chapter 7.

Getting caught up in the Drift goes right along with the trap of success. You find a path to conventional success, you get used to that set of strategies, and you get comfortable. More than that, you begin to see your current way of doing things as the *only* way to make more money, learn a new skill, or accomplish a new project. The Drift becomes second nature.

This is what I have seen with many clients and even in my own journey. You do exactly the same things you have done in the past to produce particular results. But all you'll ever achieve is more of the same.

Doing what you have always done is *not* the path to significance, or to exponential success. In fact, it is exactly what keeps you from achieving them.

>  Everyday Courage is the antidote to the Drift. It helps you break free from the current that wants to carry you along in the status quo.

This is where Everyday Courage comes in. You need this kind of courage to overcome your current level of success and strive for something bigger. Everyday Courage is the antidote to the Drift. It helps you break free from the current that wants to carry you along in the status quo.

Once you challenge those old patterns with more courageous thinking, you will see new opportunities.

What if you had a habit of acknowledging your fear and moving forward anyway? What if you had a habit of looking for something BIG and SCARY to do each and every day? What if you didn't stop yourself with old, mistaken beliefs?

When I look back at the clients I have had and the hundreds of podcast interviews I have done with ultra-successful people, I see that they have mastered the Everyday Courage part of growth. Many of them don't even realize it. It has become normal for them.

I have developed something to help you achieve the very same thing— so you can end the drift that so many people get sucked into. I call it the Courage List.

## The Courage List

Here is a very simple way to make a change in your day-to-day habits. It will help you do what scares you and achieve new levels of growth. I love to plan and list. I'm old-school, too: while I have tried apps and other tools, I still prefer using a pad or notebook to list the most important things to do today.

However, there's a key limitation. While the traditional to-do list is good for listing out what needs to get done, it leaves out the very important dimension of growing beyond where you are.

With a to-do list, we measure our day and even ourselves on how much we got done. The items there are usually tied to immediate needs—the calls we need to make, the emails we need to send, the tasks to help us complete our projects. But they usually leave out the things that challenge us, the things we fear. And they leave out those things that never seem to get done because we opt for tasks that we like to do.

What if you changed your to-do list into a Courage List? This is a list of one or two things per day that you have been avoiding because of fear—things you've resisted or delayed. Start executing the items on your list, and you'll quickly be much closer to living a fuller life.

## THE TRAP OF SUCCESS

*Check out the companion exercises on my site to get free templates and training on the Courage List:* http://thetrapofsuccess.com/companion-exercises

The items on your list could be anything, but here are a few examples:

- Scheduling a meeting with a new prospect
- Calling a meeting planner to discuss speaking at their next event
- Reaching out to a friend in your network to discuss a failure you recently encountered
- Raising your pricing
- Offering a new service
- Surveying your clients or potential clients
- Starting a new project

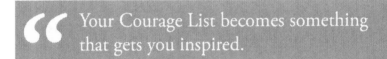

It can be anything you have been avoiding or something that makes you doubt yourself.

Your Courage List becomes something that gets you inspired. Imagine measuring your day based on your Courage List instead of your to-do list. Now imagine looking back after one month, when you have logged 30 straight days of courage.

Every single client who's tried this activity has learned something from it. The biggest benefit has been increased confidence. Some clients have also made more money. Others have booked new speaking engagements. Some have finished projects that have lingered for years. They all achieved these things by making the Courage List a daily habit.

Remember: there is not just one moment that changes you. It is all the moments stacking on top of each other that makes change happen.

It takes tremendous courage to be true to yourself and continue to grow. It takes even more courage to let go of your past ways to create something big and scary.

### Courage Will Set You Free

Most people I see in the world bargain with themselves about what comes next for them. They make excuses about why *now* is not the right time. They find themselves "stuck" in various areas of life; they're caught in the Drift. Time passes. Then one day they wake up and realize that their actions haven't lived up to their dreams.

Mark Zuckerberg's quote at the start of this chapter about choosing hope over fear really sums up what I see as the core of living a life of significance. Hope is knowing that you can achieve a future in which your current feelings of being stuck and unworthy are behind you.

Fear is all around you when you decide to live a big life—the kind of life that forces you to expand yourself. You can choose to focus on the fear, which will stop you in your tracks. Or you can focus on the hope of a better future. And that will cause you to grow.

Along the way, you will use both Pivotal Moment Courage and Everyday Courage. These are crucial aspects of playing bigger and refusing to accept what life gives you.

Creating and working through your Courage List each and every day is one of those habits that can change everything for you. Being curious about where you can become more courageous will guide you to achieving more than you even believe is possible.

In the next chapter, we'll take all of this to a higher level as we discuss how you can play to *win*.

# THE TRAP OF SUCCESS

## Questions to Inspire You

1. What is your relationship with courage?
2. Where have you faced a big fear that caused you to grow as a person?
3. How do you want to use courage in your life moving forward?
4. What are two things that you will put on your Courage List for tomorrow?

# 10 PLAYING TO WIN

**CHAPTER TEN**

Make the decision,
then make the decision
right.

-Larry Winget, Outstanding Speaker and
TV Personality

## THE TRAP OF SUCCESS

What do Warren Buffett, Oprah Winfrey, Mark Cuban, Jeff Bezos, Richard Branson, Michael Jordan, Arianna Huffington, Sara Blakely, and Mark Zuckerberg have in common? Besides being extremely wealthy? For one, they think differently than most of us. I don't know them personally, but having read a lot about all of them and having coached many other highly successful people, I know that reaching their levels of success is because they see opportunities that most people don't see. This is the reason they are consistently on the forefront of business news, and icons of the business community.

 The "inner game" is the basis for achieving exponential success and creating significance.

The titans of business don't play the same game that we do. They are super-smart, and that is important, but they also think *differently* than the common business owner. Thinking differently includes terms like "mindset," "psychology," and "mental toughness." As I did earlier in the book, I will use the term "inner game" to encompass these ideas as I discuss the thinking patterns that shape the actions we take or don't take in life.

The "inner game" is the basis for achieving exponential success and creating significance. The way you think determines the way you see the world and see yourself. In this chapter, we dive deep into the inner game to uncover ways that will allow you to continually grow.

Here are just a few reasons why the inner game is so important:

- If your thinking is stunted by the past or by insecurity, it will limit your growth.
- If your thinking is not able to adjust to new opportunities, you will not navigate change well.
- If your thinking does not allow you to filter out the good and great opportunities to find the best ones, you will struggle to keep up.

I could go on and on. The way you think determines your ability to create a new future.

## Ron Dod's Story: The Inner Game in Real Life

A little while back, I was working with a new client of mine. His name is Ron Dod. Ron was running a marketing agency, Grey Umbrella Marketing, in Atlanta. (In 2016 the company merged with Visiture in Charleston, S.C.) Ron's business was in good shape in terms of revenue, with a heap of happy clients. I remember him bragging about a 96 percent retention rate.

Ron didn't seem to need a coach. He was smart and had a drive inside him to figure out whatever came across his path. (This isn't uncommon: Most of my clients don't need a coach. They *want* a coach to challenge them to continuously grow.)

In our initial conversations, I could tell that Ron would be great to work with. He badly wanted to grow his company. When I say badly, it seemed like he was aching inside to go beyond his current limits.

I usually assess how much someone wants to change as a barometer for the success they will have with coaching. This is really about answering "Are they coachable?" The reality is, not everyone wants to grow inside. Not everyone wants to change. Many people will say they do, but few are willing to do the inner work to make it happen.

Ron, though, was ready. Ron wanted to shift his business to a new path. Ron wanted to grow fast—really fast.

The problem was that he didn't have the right strategy for massive growth. He had a strategy of sorts, though, and he was working it. Ron's strategy was "get clients."

This strategy is the recipe for growing incrementally. Ron could grow his business one client at a time, hold onto the clients he had, and amass enough revenue to make a good living. That's what most business owners do. It works if all you want is incremental success, but it's a poor way to achieve exponential success. With this approach, your work becomes more about wrestling day in and day out to get clients and to make them happy. Put out today's fires—rinse and repeat.

I can remember seeing Ron's genius when he couldn't. Ron wanted to grow his revenue and company so badly that he took on any clients that came his way. And that was his problem: he had so much desire and drive, but was thinking the wrong way about how to achieve his goals. The way he thought about his business—his inner game—was limiting his growth.

Early on in my work with Ron, we had a tough conversation. It wasn't about sales, or even his business per se. Rather, we talked about the frustrations and struggles he experienced while running his business. We just needed to get clear about what was going on inside him relative to the work he was doing. He was disappointed with the day-to-day struggles of the business. He had bunches of clients and offered them many services. In fact, he saw that as his only choice.

I challenged that thinking. "Really? You don't have any other choice?"

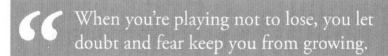

> When you're playing not to lose, you let doubt and fear keep you from growing.

"No, I have to make money to pay my team and pay my bills." Ron declared.

Ron was trapped in his success. He was operating his business with a mindset of "playing not to lose." When you're playing not to lose, you let doubt and fear keep you from growing.

He didn't see it. How could he? He was living it. It is hard to see what is really going on when you are down in the middle of your life and your business. It's not just that you feel too busy to step back and gain a different perspective; there is also an emotional attachment to the way it has always been done. It's another form of the *homeostasis* we discussed earlier.

Our conversation continued to dig into Ron's daily frustration with the business. Then, I shifted to talk about the future of the business. If it continued this way, what would happen? I could see by the look on his face that for once he was stepping back from leading a company to really look at what was going on. As soon as he did that, Ron didn't see the current path as the best one for long-term growth. His eyes lit up with a new intention for his business and himself.

Ron's skills and talent had gotten him to this point. But to go further without driving himself into the ground, he would need to look at his business through a new lens.

We continued to discuss his options, brainstorming at the highest levels of his business strategy. We assessed the different avenues he could take to build the business so that he could go beyond his current realm of success, achieve exponential success, and build something of significance.

Ron played along during this part of the conversation. I urged him to dream big—to remove the traditional limitations. He was uncomfortable with some of the things we discussed; I remember how his body language changed in reaction to some of the ideas. Yet we kept going. We uncovered a number of ways for him to have the business he wanted *and* the life he wanted.

Ron began to light up. You could see the energy in his smile and hear the joy in his voice. He began to see a realm of possibility that was not there before. Ron got excited about being a market leader and thought leader in his industry. I think that's what Ron wanted all along, but he had fallen into operating the company like those who had gone before him in the world of marketing.

177

## THE TRAP OF SUCCESS

This was the moment when Ron made a shift. He was ready to let go of the old way; his inner game had changed. It's not always that quick for my clients, but when the inner game does change, all the other stuff becomes easy. I say "other stuff" because running a business involves many talents and skills, and it involves finding the right strategy and implementing it with a lot of attention to detail. Ron had most of this; we just worked to channel it toward what he really wanted.

That was the starting point for Ron to grow his company by *412 percent* in twelve months. It's almost unreal for a business that's already successful to grow that much, that fast. But the revenue wasn't all that changed. Because Ron was now playing to win, he was willing to break away from what wasn't working—or what *was* working but keeping him on the old incremental track—to find a new path. We removed frustrating services, and even frustrating clients. We analyzed the markets Ron wanted to focus on and developed a strategy that played to his strengths.

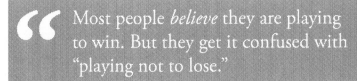

> Most people *believe* they are playing to win. But they get it confused with "playing not to lose."

### What Is Playing to Win?

You've heard "play to win" before. Most people *believe* they are playing to win. But they get it confused with "playing not to lose." This may seem like I'm mincing words, but I'm actually talking about an entirely different approach. It is a different way to think.

When you reach a level of success where you start to play it safe, you stop growing. By contrast, when you play to win, you continue to grow to meet new opportunities. You push beyond the edge of comfort.

Once you have decided to get uncomfortable, you can use the concept of playing to win to challenge yourself and expand your comfort zone.

Let's make it perfectly clear: playing to win *requires* being uncomfortable. When you play to win, you commit to no longer play it safe. That takes courage and confidence, and it implies pushing yourself into painful new territory.

When your business reaches a plateau of sorts, you have a choice. You always have a choice. You can accept your success as final. You've "made it." Or you can look inside yourself to decide what's next and come up with something that scares you in a good way. Playing to win means having the willingness to let go of past achievements so you can gun for something bigger and more innovative.

I know these feelings well. My sports tour business reached the plateau I'm describing in 2006. I had just had the biggest event of my life—the 2006 World Cup in Germany. I worked with a variety of sources for tickets, one of whom was a South African man with years of experience. He offered me thousands of tickets, but I was scared at first. I had done a few deals with him before, but nothing like the size of this one.

So I passed on his first offer—it was too uncomfortable for me. I took the safe route. Near Christmas of 2005, I reached out to him again to see what was happening. He had sold nearly every ticket he had. He offered me 20 tickets to one match. Yes, just 20—when I was used to dealing in hundreds or thousands of tickets at a time. But I took a chance and purchased them, despite the risk of sending money to South Africa to a man I had met once before in Athens during the 2004 Olympics. I would make $15,000 if these tickets came in, or I would lose $3,000 if they didn't. With a quick evaluation, I accepted the risk.

As he and I talked during the course of the next six months, I slowly bought more tickets from him as they came available. Ultimately, I sent him $50,000 with no contract and only a promise. I was nervous. Or you could say I was uncomfortable—really uncomfortable—but I decided to play to win. In other words, I was all in.

Before the meeting with him to pick up the tickets, I was a wreck. I had heartburn from the stress. After I had landed in Amsterdam with my wife a few days earlier, the pain in my chest grew. I was thinking about how to go to the hospital in a country where I didn't have medical coverage. My wife was concerned for me, and I think I was delirious, too.

We continued on to Germany. The pain and stress continued until I got the call from the South African. We had only exchanged emails for the previous few days, but now he had arrived in Frankfurt as planned. He invited me for beer at his hotel. The pain got worse as I made my way to the lobby of his hotel. When I saw him there, the pain in my chest vanished almost immediately.

Over a round of beers, we laughed and discussed details of the delivery of the tickets to me. The pain came back in a milder form; I guess my body knew that the stress was not over. I wouldn't feel better until I had my tickets in my hands.

My South African contact asked me for a favor. He wanted me to join him at the FIFA corporate office the next day to claim our tickets, he would need help to count and sort thousands of tickets. When the time came, we took a train and walked into a fancy office building in Frankfurt to claim his tickets. After waiting for security clearance and going through polite introductions with ticketing officials for FIFA, security guards wheeled in boxes of tickets—big boxes. We had to sort through four of them to ensure we had received the South African's entire order.

In a matter of minutes, I was counting thousands of tickets to the biggest sporting event in the world. The tickets were worth millions. This was the scale at which the South African operated. I was thinking about what I had missed out on because I was scared. My true shift to playing to win started in that moment. I'm glad I changed my thinking.

By the way, I purchased only 150 tickets from the South African. That was a mere handful compared to the four boxes that I had just counted.

Did being exposed to that much money change me? Or did the decision to play a different game change me? I believe it was about the decision. I made a commitment like I had never done before.

Meanwhile, I had $50,000 invested, with the plan to turn it into $200,000. The gamble was big, but it paid off. After that, playing to win gave me a much bigger payday: I took the momentum from that initial deal into the rest of the 2006 World Cup and made more than $450,000 profit in eight weeks.

The decision to play to win takes your drive to a higher level. You start going for what is hard and not backing down from challenges. You meet new opportunities and decide how to make them work for you. When you play to win, you aren't looking for the easy way.

Keep in mind, though: Playing to win is **not** about pushing hard at all cost. Playing to win is about deciding what will fulfill your deepest existential need, then creating the circumstances necessary to achieve it. Playing to win requires commitment, confidence, and self-awareness in service of growth and excellence. It is the starting point to greatness.

> True significance only comes when you decide to operate at your highest level. Settling for anything else means achieving only a shadow of your potential.

### Playing Not To Lose Is All Too Common

I am so lucky in my day-to-day interactions with business owners and leaders: I get to see behind the curtains of success—and even significance—to see how people think. I get to witness their level of confidence and limiting beliefs, too. This is important, because it allows me to evaluate what works and what doesn't when it comes to building businesses and creating value in this world.

## THE TRAP OF SUCCESS

From all of this, I've learned that business success (heck, *life* success) does not happen for those who are playing not to lose. And true significance only comes when you decide to operate at your highest level. Settling for anything else means achieving only a shadow of your potential.

Playing not to lose is about protecting what you have rather than striving for the next level. It's about maintaining the status quo. In business, playing not to lose shows up in making small incremental gains. While it can be good to increase profits and gain market share by small steps, it often means you are missing opportunities to make big leaps in your business.

I see it all the time: business owners who have amassed a level of financial security—even financial freedom—in their businesses, yet who hold themselves back from what they really want. If you're in this situation, you likely have financial security to do what you want, but you may not have the time to do it. Financial freedom comes when you have both the money and the time.

You can also see the playing-not-to-lose mentality in employees who dream of a new and bigger future. Sometimes the future is inside the company and sometimes it is outside. Many times they dream of starting their own businesses. Yet they are trapped in the limited model of success that comes with being someone else's employee.

The truth is that, whether you're an employee or an entrepreneur, professional growth is a constant balance of doing what you must do to keep going—to pay your bills, support your family, and so on—and making the bold moves required to expand your boundaries and fulfill you as a person.

I remember having financial freedom in my sports tour business. I had plenty of money in the bank so I could live life with little concern. On top of that, I had tons of free time for more than eight months of the year. Some months were very demanding, but that's to be expected when you're running a business dependent on events like the World Cup or the Olympics.

Once I had financial freedom, I started to think about my next move in business. As I've discussed in earlier chapters, I wanted more than money. I wanted to make a difference. I felt a drive to create something innovative that had a worldly purpose. Yet I held myself back. I wouldn't make the bold moves required to do something really groundbreaking.

I was playing not to lose...and you know how that turned out. (If you skipped the "Introduction" in this book, you might want to go back and read it now.)

Part of why I expose my own success and failure is so you can see similar patterns within your own decisions. Then you can make clearer choices and play the game the way you really want to play it.

Now that we understand playing not to lose, we can take a deeper look at playing to win.

## How Do You "Play to Win"?

In my coaching, I have worked with hundreds of people on changing their thinking so they can build their businesses differently. I have seen some of them refuse to change, but I have also seen many change in an instant. My goal here is to codify the key aspects of the shift in thinking that supports a play-to-win approach.

Remember, this is about more than making tons of money; it is about committing yourself to a life in which you feel like your work matters and you matter in the world. It's about living up to your calling or highest potential.

We are going to explore five areas as a starting point. There are more than just these five, but once you understand these, you can use them to expand into other areas.

183

## THE TRAP OF SUCCESS

- Focus
- Commitment
- Self-Confidence
- Self-Awareness
- Abundance

### Focus

Focus seems to be the first stumbling block to growth. Focus is more than just your ability to sit down and complete a task, which we might more appropriately call "productivity." As I'm defining it here, focus is about your ability to clarify what you want to do and who you want to serve with what you do.

As I've said, most people don't have a clear idea about these things. Since this is common for business owners, lack of focus is a pervasive problem among small businesses. (But larger businesses can also struggle with it.)

Regardless of your company's size, the idea of casting a wide net and seeing what happens is a huge mistake. In the early days of a company, many people rationalize that they need to take any client who has money—the same way Ron Dod tried to grow his business. I have had that conversation more times than I can count.

The *right* strategy is to be clear about who your ideal clients are and how you serve them. It is focused—I mean crystal clear. If it is fuzzy to you, it will be fuzzy to your clients.

You have to decide where you want to focus. I have interviewed hundreds of successful business owners and entrepreneurial leaders. They have shared some insights with me over the last few years that will help you. The most common statement that comes up on my podcast is "You can't be all things to all people." I know you must have have heard this before. In practice, it means that, if you cast that wide net to see what you catch, and if you take all the clients that come to you, you can severely hurt your business. It is a paradox. You think you want all the clients you can get, but a random set of clients does more harm than good.

When I interview people about their path to success and significance, I start essentially every episode with the question, "Who do you serve?" Besides giving the guest a chance to explain what they do, I'm alerting my audience so the right people can pay attention and others can tune out. (Remember: It's a *good* thing to limit your audience, or your client base, to only the most relevant people.)

It's easy to look at those further down the path of business success, realize they have a broader audience or reach than you do, and then believe that a broad audience is the path to growth.

Well, let me the be bearer of bad news: That is wrong. Dead wrong.

I have researched and analyzed this particular aspect of business— finding your niche—by interviewing dozens of authors on marketing. This one aspect of business is so often ignored or forgotten that it is a killer to success.

The fear that goes with this is one of "limiting yourself" and "losing opportunities." Some even call it FOMO, for Fear Of Missing Out.

Don't worry about "missing out" on the clients or opportunities that are irrelevant to your success and significance. The journey to building a profitable and repeatable venture is fueled by your ability to focus.

Focus has other aspects, too. You have to discover the few things that matter so you can figure them out and master them. You can't master everything.

Mastery is narrow and specific. It is not broad. Mozart did not master all forms of music. The Beatles played their style of music—not others'. Sure, there are exceptions to this, like the ultimate Renaissance man Leonardo Da Vinci. If you are as talented at Leonardo, you can safely ignore this part of the book. Otherwise, lean into it and soak in the importance of "focus."

Focus is also about saying "no" to the bad ideas...and the merely good ideas, too. Warren Buffett has said that out of 100 ideas presented to him, he says "no" to 99 of them. That is how he ensures continued success.

I hope this is sinking in. Just in case it's not, let's look at a lesson from one of the young titans of business. Gary Vaynerchuk, co-founder of Vaynermedia and *New York Times* bestselling author of many books, believes that one teachable element of success is *depth*. As he puts it, "the world is really about depth, not width." He goes on to say that success in business requires doing things that are meaningful—not wide. He calls it the "Depth Game." The reality that Gary sees is this: many people say they believe in depth, yet the way they operate is wide. Depth is what creates the impact that drives real growth. Width is a shallow approach to growth.

The truth is, successful people say "No" to most things and "Hell, yes!" to a select few. When you make the decision to go deep and focus, you are establishing a play-to-win mindset. Playing the inner game this way is a game changer.

Focus on what will keep you growing, not on what keeps you safe. You can't be pulled in many directions and expect to be conscious of your personal choices. Distraction is your enemy when you're playing to win.

### Commitment

The term commitment is tossed around way too lightly in our conversations. When you are playing to win, commitment is not some loosey-goosey concept. In fact, commitment is something that the people driving hard to create a new future use sparingly. They don't commit to projects or people half-heartedly. They have an absolute sense of commitment, and they don't take it lightly.

I had Larry Winget, a six-time *New York Times* and *Wall Street Journal* bestselling author, on the podcast. We came to a part of the conversation about commitment that has stuck with me. We were discussing what it takes to be successful. Larry's view of the world centers on the motto "Take Personal Responsibility." When others take personal responsibility for their debt, their children, and their work, they are empowered to do something about it. However, it is all too common to blame someone else or play the role of victim.

Larry shared a concept about commitment that still rings in my ears:

*"But when it doesn't start to go well, commitment waivers. You see true commitment never waivers. I'm not committed to my wife only when I like her. I've got to be committed to my wife and our marriage even when we are in the middle of an ugly place in our lives. I am not committed to my kids when they are making me happy. I am committed to them when they are being idiots, too."*
—**Larry Winget**, Multiple Bestselling Author and News Commentator

When you play to win, your commitment does not waiver. You find a way to make it work. You find a way to keep going.

Go back to the other quote from Larry that I used to start this chapter:

*"Make the decision, then make the decision right."*
—**Larry Winget,** Entrepreneur who Sees the Funny Everywhere

This is so simple and so powerful. I have quoted Larry on this one idea hundreds of times. We have a tendency to over complicate our lives. We overthink all too often. Larry's view on this is to do what it takes to make a decision, and then do what it takes make that decision pay off.

Life and business are really that simple: make a decision, and then *commit* to backing up that decision. The flipside of that is not a real commitment, but a constant back-and-forth. You have likely encountered someone who's trapped in that kind of indecision...it irritated you, right? Don't be that person. Make a commitment and stick to it.

Commitment is part of play-to-win thinking. Don't waver on your commitment to your decisions.

### Self-Confidence

Believing in yourself is what allows for growth, despite now knowing how or having the resources to accomplish something new. Belief is the first thing to come. Before your decisions are made, you believe it is possible and you believe you can do it. That's what starts everything.

There are, of course, those who timidly approach life. I call this "tiptoeing" into something; it rarely works out in the absence of a clear sense of confidence.

The other side of confidence is being doubtful. Doubt arises from uncertainty and fear. It comes from the inner critic that wants to prevent change. That inner critic is the channel for fear, heard in the common refrain "You're not good enough." Living in a mode of doubt is unlikely to give you the life and business you want. In fact, this negative self-talk will directly prevent you from attaining what you really want.

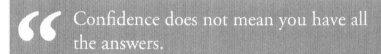

"Confidence does not mean you have all the answers.

Professor and collegiate soccer coach Dr. Ivan Joseph shared his views on confidence in a TEDx talk. He said that when you lose sight of or belief in yourself, you are done. Dr. Joseph defined confidence as "the ability to believe in yourself to accomplish any task, no matter the odds, no matter the difficulty, no matter the adversity."

Self-confidence is a skill. It is built by repetition, repetition, repetition. Confidence grows from practice. It requires cultivating resilience and persistence. Dr. Joseph understands the self-confidence gives you the power to create your future. Confidence does not mean you have all the answers. It does not mean you have a plan or the step-by-step blueprint yet.

There are moments that will shake your confidence. That's a common experience, and we all have to choose whether or not to stay in that place. You can rise above it.

Back in 2010, I lost everything: my business, my money, my house, and my confidence. I was a shadow of who I had been before I hit rock bottom. My doubt was epic. I questioned every decision I made and struggled to see the real me. I had to find my confidence again before making a comeback.

My example may be extreme, but you have likely felt something similar in some part of your life. But if I can bounce back and regain my confidence, so can you. You have to believe in yourself and build confidence in your abilities and your drive to find a way.

Thoughts influence actions. If you don't believe in yourself, others will doubt you, too. Creating value in the world requires self-confidence.

## Self-Awareness

When you understand self-awareness, you have the capacity to set boundaries for yourself. You define what you can do and what you will do. Self-awareness means cultivating an intimate understanding of your strengths and knowledge of your own emotions and energy, which influence your capacity to meet life's great moments.

When you are self-aware, you have clarity about where you are going and what you believe. You show up with intention for life's important moments. You have a deep sense of presence, with people you love and with those you don't.

Being self-aware causes you to bring your authentic self to the world.

## THE TRAP OF SUCCESS

You don't numb it with drugs, alcohol, food, or materialism. You are not keen to escape life with distractions. You don't block your emotions. Those who are self-aware can endure the painful moments of life and operate in a way that that helps them move forward.

By contrast, those who are intent on blocking out reality and running away from life because it does not go their way are not self-aware. In fact, they are fleeing self-awareness.

Being self-aware includes understanding what you are tolerating in your life. Most people are not tuned into what they are tolerating; it's invisible to them.

Merely "tolerating" something is the feeling you get when that thing is not the way you expect it to be, not the way you want it to be. For instance, you may want a given circumstance to be different, but you have grown so accustomed to it that you look past it. You think it's okay as it is. But the real truth is that a part of you feels disatisfied each time you experience that inadequate state of affairs. For one person, it is the smacking of your coworker's gum that grates on your nerves, and for another it is the piles of stuff that sit around the house, always out of place.

When you tolerate something, you are letting it undermine your self-awareness. In the simplest of terms, your "tolerations" zap your energy.

Your self-awareness keeps you tuned into your identity, which allows you to make decisions based on a candid assessment of your strengths and weaknesses. Having a keen sense of self-awareness is required for you to play to win.

### Abundance
Focusing on what you don't have is "lack" thinking. Believing that you have to grab it all and hold on tight is also lack thinking. When you see opportunities as limited, you are focused on what you don't have—what you *lack*.

Abundance thinking is the opposite and allows you to go beyond the norms. When you have an abundance mindset, you don't see competition, you see the opportunity for all.

For example, there are those who constantly think, "I don't have the money to _____." *Lack!* Those who think from a place of abundance, however, ask themselves, "How can I make this happen?"

Too many people really have no sense of the role this thinking— *abundance* versus *lack*—plays in their lives. It is a blind spot that does not allow them to recognize how they really think. You can notice it when you listen to the words they use. Do they use "shoulda, coulda, woulda" in describing their future?

Let me give you an example: "I should..." is not language of abundance. The statement is wrapped in limitations. Compare it to the words "I do... " or "I am..." or "I choose..." It is a small change in word choice, but its ability to generate new results in life is remarkable.

Making the shift to abundance starts by changing your point of focus. Thinking about what you don't have will only get you more of that not-having. Thinking about the opportunities available to you will make them more attainable.

Playing to win means seeing the opportunity instead of the challenges.

## Winning on Your Own Terms

Let me be clear—you don't have to become as rich or famous as the titans of business that I listed in the opening of this chapter. In fact, I think that you can only achieve significance if you are authentically being *you*. And you can't be you if you try to emulate someone else.

*Significance* requires figuring out whether you have been playing to win or playing not to lose. Be honest with yourself. You can't grow if you take only a shallow look into your past. Pull back the layers that you have amassed over the years, remove the masks that protect you, and get real with yourself.

If a transformation is necessary, you can begin with an honest look at your levels of:

- **Focus** — knowing clearly where you are going and whom you are serving
- **Commitment** — separating weak from strong commitments
- **Self-confidence** — assessing your self-worth
- **Self-awareness** — knowing your true identity
- **Abundance** — seeing the opportunities ahead of you instead of the lack in your life

The inner game lays the foundation for the steps you must take to create significance.

In the next chapter, we will explore how to test what you do to find out what's truly essential in your world.

### Questions to Inspire You

1. Over the last six months, think of one area in your life where you have been playing not to lose?
2. Where can you see that you were playing to win?
3. How would describe your inner game now?

# 11

# TESTING THE ESSENTIAL

A little less conversation, a little more action please...

-Elvis Presley, American Music Icon and King of Rock and Roll

## THE TRAP OF SUCCESS

Let's get real.

Life is busy. It pulls you in so many directions that you just can't seem to control your day. Family is always on the go, and our professional lives require us to do more and more each year.

Your to-do list is more than likely a big source of stress. For some, it acts more as an engine churning out guilt than it serves as a productivity tool. You have more on the list than you have the capacity to do. Yet you keep adding to the list, and you try new ways to handle it all.

On top of all this, in the last decade our lives have changed dramatically. Social media has exploded, and not just for the young. The fastest-growing segment of social media users are those older than 60. It's not that social media is bad per se, but it has changed the way we interact with each other, and for many it has become a huge time suck.

And since the release of the first iPhone in 2007, we now carry around a pocket full of distractions—email, socializing, gaming, watching cat videos, playing with apps, and on and on. For most of us, it is a natural thing to pull out the phone whenever there is the slightest pause in our daily activities, including when we're out with family and friends. We even watch TV with our phones and tablets at our fingertips. *Fortune Magazine* published a *Bank of America* study which found that 71 percent of people with smartphones sleep with their phones beside them. In New York, 96 percent of those with a smartphone check it at least once per hour.

For most of you, technology has not allowed you to be in more control. It has provided more reasons to not do what you want to be doing.

Another contributing factor to our busy lives is that the desire to learn is compelling us to read more, watch more videos, and consume more information. With all this new information, we are getting less and less done. It is easy to justify that this is good for us, but frankly there is an overload of "learning" and a serious deficit of **doing**.

194

*"We are drowning in information, yet we are starving for wisdom."*
—**E.O. Wilson**, Author and Father of Sociobiology

We are starving for real wisdom, so I hope you will take what I share with you here as a way to go beyond just more information.

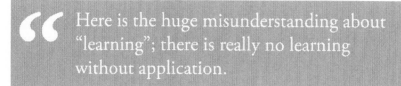

Here is the huge misunderstanding about "learning"; there is really no learning without application.

The advent of tech in our lives has caused us to get stuck in information consumption and hindered our ability to apply the knowledge we take in.

Are you consuming more than you create? Are you watching others more than living your own life?

Here is the huge misunderstanding about "learning"; there is really no learning without application. This means that learning without doing is just a time suck.

If you're like most people, you are likely suffering in your ability to filter out the essential from the trivial. According to the U.S. Department of Labor, in 2014 Americans averaged 3 hours and 35 minutes of daily TV watching. And the U.S. market is seeing a staggering 4.7 hours per day per person on smartphones, according to *Informate Mobile Intelligence.*

This problem is also compounded by the attention we pay to the *immediate* instead of the *important.* We have a seemingly endless list of options for things to do for every project or challenge we are facing. We tell ourselves that this is the way it is now. We justify it. We make excuses about it. We rationalize how important all of our projects are to our progress.

## THE TRAP OF SUCCESS

I'm just like you on this, too. I have struggled to balance and juggle life and business. With my coaching business and all of the possible opportunities in today's world, I have been through periods of severe overload and overwhelm. I am a speaker, writer, podcaster, coach, father, husband, son, and friend. I want to be healthy. I want to be organized. I have a drive to move forward, and that makes me create long lists of things to do. I make up stories in my head about why I'm the only one who can do them. I get stressed for not getting it all done. In the past, I have refused to let go of the "trivial many" to focus on the "essential few."

I have worked hard to learn to let go of all the trivial things so I can work hard on the most important projects within my business. I have lived inside that struggle for months at a time until I consciously break free from those bonds.

Is it the same for you? Your days are filled with opportunities to make more money, get more traction, or develop the people around you. In fact, you probably have more opportunities than time. I say "probably" here, but I know that this is the case for so many people that it has become a way of life.

The problem is that rarely do we focus on the most important opportunities. Most people don't have a solid filtering system that allows them to focus on the essential items. Some just don't have the discipline to say "No." Either way, it's easy to be pulled in many directions.

It is just not easy to let go of it all.

> " Giving in to all the stuff in our lives is the winding road to the status quo.

### Seeing, Testing, Filtering
With the plethora of tech distractions and the lack a strong filtering

196

mechanism for what's important, you are sucked into the day. You are swirled around by stuff, and while it may be stuff you need to do, it leaves no room for what must be done in our personal and professional lives if we want to achieve success or significance.

In fact, giving in to all the *stuff* in our lives is the winding road to the status quo. It puts you right in the middle of the pack with most people working hard to break free from their current level of growth.

Creating exponential success and especially significance requires you to filter out distractions and decide what is most important so you can act with intensity and commitment.

In this chapter, I'm going to dive into two pillars—seeing things as a test and filtering to the essential—that are crucial for getting more done and getting the right things done.

Bear with me here before you say, "Yeah, yeah—get more done, and do the right things." If you look at what I share with you and reflexively say "I've heard it before"...you will continue to get what you have gotten.

In the pages that follow, I share an approach that has changed the lives of my clients—as well as my own. It builds on the best of my research from hundreds of interviews on the *Leaders in the Trenches* podcast, and from the daily experience of working with clients in my coaching business.

I have seen my clients change their entire work capacity with these strategies. Learn to prioritize your next steps with these essential strategies to growth. It will concentrate your energy on the most important actions that have the highest payoff for your business and life.

### Getting Down to the Essentials

I have talked about focusing on the most important things. No doubt you have heard this before, but you likely struggle to apply it to your life. Be honest here—no one is looking: raise your hand if you have too much going on right now and aren't sure how to slow down to figure out what is most important.

I am smiling as I write this, because the same thing applies to me in spades. Who knew a book would take this long to write, edit, and publish? I have opportunities coming from many angles. I have felt the pressure of this in my whole body. The flood of opportunities is evidence of my years of experience with clients and building my team, so I'm not complaining. It has just gotten harder over the years to stay true and focused on what is most important. This includes family, friends, and business. It also includes my health.

Finding the essential is really a filtering process or system to remove the trivial and even the "good" stuff from your daily focus. I say "good" here because there is a reason why it's on your list in the first place. It is likely good for you or your business. But "good" does not automatically mean "important." Good is rarely *essential*.

The process of *removal* is really the key here. It hurts to remove all the things you want to do and leave yourself with only the most important elements. But if you do it well, you remove *all* tasks and projects that are distractions to leave yourself with only the essential ones.

When you prioritize your next project by discovering the essential path to growth, you actually free yourself from the juggling—and the lies of multitasking.

Yes, I said it. Multitasking has proven to fail with all complex and thinking tasks. Sure, you can talk on the phone and drive (well, some people can). You can watch TV and fold clothes (my ten-year-old struggles with this one, but does his best). But you can't multitask your way through anything that requires you to be creative and innovative. And I do mean you *cannot*: the neuroscientists have confirmed that the human brain simply is not wired that way.

Learning how to separate the essential from the non-essential is critical to your progress. You know that if the bulk of your time is spent on non-essential tasks—those that don't have the highest payoff for your professional and personal life—you will not accomplish what you want. You won't be who you want to be.

You can't "nonessential" your way to significance.

## Finding the Essential

I interviewed Greg McKeown about this for my podcast. He literally wrote the book on being an essentialist. Greg is the *New York Times* bestselling author of *Essentialism: The Disciplined Pursuit of Less,* which is about how to live a more purposeful, focused, and intentional life.

Essentialism is the art of discerning between external noise and internal voice. It's not about making a tactical list to manage your tasks and your time. It's more than that. It's a mindset—a way of life.

Greg's book goes deep to help you filter through all the things you *could* do to find those few things that are most powerful and important. I highly recommend the book if you want to go further into that important subject.

Ultimately, my take on this is quite simple. Are you willing to take a disciplined look at what is important and what merely seems important to determine what's truly essential?

Once you do find the essential, you have to let go of everything else.

Greg shared a practical and actionable exercise with me that is powerful—if you have the courage to apply it.

1. Take a few minutes every day to make an essential list of six important things to do.
2. Place them in order of priority.
3. Cross out the bottom five. Take the top item and do as much as you can to get it done.
4. Then move on to the next item on your list.

199

## THE TRAP OF SUCCESS

Okay, four steps. It's that simple—and simple is best if you want to make it work.

I will be honest with you. I was recording the call for my podcast with Greg and started to write down the six things that I wanted to do before the end of the day. Then he gave the power punch by saying "Now cross out the bottom five."

I had an ache in my gut when he said it. I retracted back into my normal pattern of thinking. I thought for a second about how important the other five things were to my business. The mindset of an essentialist allows you to defer everything else that is not the *most* important. You learn that you must finish that one thing before moving on to the next.

The more common approach is to switch back and forth in the day among different projects and tasks, which makes it hard to keep your concentration on the single most important thing. As I write this, I know I must finish this chapter before eating breakfast—and I am hungry. I'm even more hungry as I write about it. But every fiber in my body says I must finish this before I can take the time to eat.

Finding your essential work every single day allows you to develop the habit of finding the most important projects in your life. Although this book is mainly about business growth, this specific habit applies to life in general, too.

When you let go of all the other stuff that occupies your mind, you can concentrate on the one project or task that allows real progress. It makes it easier to remove the distractions of life and focus on what's truly important.

I just love the following question posed by Gary Keller and Jay Papasan, which is also about finding the essential—that one project to pull you toward significance:

*"What is the one thing I can do such that by doing it everything else will be easier or unnecessary?"*
—**Gary Keller** and **Jay Papasan**, Notable Authors and Trail Blazers

I interviewed Jay Papasan for the *Leaders in the Trenches* podcast to discover the basis for this one question. He explained that their study of thousands of Keller Williams real estate agents revealed that a few agents got more done, day in and day out, by following the principles that Keller and Papasan subsequently laid out in their book, *The One Thing*. When I reflect on that single question from Gary and Jay, I see that it goes beyond finding the priorities of what is first and what comes next. It allows you to identify a single task that has a profound impact in all that you do. This is what it means to find the "essential."

Everything just laid out in this section is about creating a filtering system to find out what is most critical in your journey to significance and greater success. Once you have found the essential, you must take action, which means testing your ideas against reality.

### It's Just a Test

Don't get caught in the trap of waiting for the "right" time" to act, or waiting for conditions to be *perfect*, because that time and those conditions will never exist. Waiting for them to arrive only creates more excuses that become enemies to growth. Instead, you want to start *before* you're ready. The feeling of not being ready is really just fear talking to you—your inner critic holding you back again.

Having the courage to move forward despite the fear will pay off for you. There is really no such thing as being completely ready. Young couples who wait to be ready to have a child may find themselves waiting forever.

Waiting to be ready in your business to take a big and bold move is a killer to growth.

Successful organizations and successful people **take action**. They create a new future by moving forward. Those on a journey to significance are likewise taking action on the essential.

Let's look at action from a different perspective—one you may not have tried before:

### What if your actions are really just tests?

Yes, tests. What if your next step or your next task is a test? If you see it as a test—an experiment that you are running and observing—you will want to know the answers to it.

This is a mental reframing that causes you to take action out of pure curiosity. If you are curious about something, you are pulled to figure out the answer.

### Everything Is a Test

I borrow this perspective from a coaching client of mine you've already met. That client, Jason Swenk, has been extremely successful in creating a business where he is the expert and thought leader in his market. He works with digital agencies to scale their businesses.

He attributes much of his success to a mindset that he has toward action. "Everything is a test" is the exact phrase he used to describe to me his journey to creating a seven-figure business. I am super proud of Jason, who has brought himself so far since I first started helping him define his business (as discussed in Chapter 7).

Jason grew his business with tremendous speed all on his own. No investors. No loans. Just him taking action daily to create his business and his life with full intention.

Now Jason's business is doing extremely well, with multiple revenue streams. He got there by testing one piece at a time. He has tested and fine-tuned each of those pieces to create a steady flow of achievements. He even breaks some things on purpose to see what will happen—everything is just a test.

Jason didn't get held up with waiting for things to be perfect.

## The Hypothesis and the Test

The concept of testing goes back to the scientific method you probably learned in your high school days. Don't break into a sweat if you hated science because the concept is simple. Look at what you are doing and turn it into a statement called a hypothesis. Then, look at the statement to see how you can test if you are right.

E.g. In creating the book cover for this book, I believed that the one you are holding was the right one for me. My hypothesis was "the orange cover was best for this book." I looked at my options and turned it all into a test for my clients, my audience, and my friends to select their favorite. I had hundreds of people give feedback. I turned it into a test. I selected the cover that got 55.3% of the votes.

Honestly, I did stress a bit to make sure it was right until I remember that I had to turn it into a test to move forward. In other words, this really works when you use it.

Looking at your projects and tasks as a "test" will help you keep moving.

You observe the results. If it fails, you rework it (going back to my example, time to redesign the "book cover") and repeat the process.

I know: simple. It's supposed to be simple.

Looking at your business and life as a series of tests allows you to break down your challenges into manageable parts and move forward in an iterative way. This removes perfection and procrastination from what you are doing so you can focus on making *progress*.

Right now I won't unpack the need so many of us have for things to be perfect, or why procrastination has such a pull on us. Instead, I will give you a story involving more of my clients that underscores the importance of taking steady action to test and learn.

# THE TRAP OF SUCCESS

## Low-Hanging Fruit

I was working with a small group of clients—four business owners in the same industry. I wanted to get them a quick win, so I offered them a way to boost income right away and with minimal resistance.

It goes like this: look back over the last six to twelve months and make a list of all the people you did business with. These are past clients for whom the project is already finished or the product is already delivered. Add to that list the other prospects you interacted with, but who didn't hire you, whether because they chose another company or they delayed their decision.

The hypothesis for this test is that reaching out to people who you already know—and who have clearly and recently been in the market for what you offer—would be the quickest way to increase revenues with a new project, or else get a referral. This is a great exercise in part because it's so quick and so direct, so take three minutes to make your own list right now.

Okay, you should have a list of 15 or more people that you can reach out to with a thoughtful message. I find that phone is best, but you can use email, too. This is your "low-hanging fruit list."

I asked these four business owners to reach out to each person on their low-hanging fruit lists. No one had any problem with the assignment. They all accepted it and thought it would be an easy way to get more business. Everyone had one week to run this test.

(Side note: it's amazing how few business owners have a regular strategy like the low-hanging fruit list for nurturing relationships.)

Okay—the outcome. Are you curious about what happened with this test?

First, three of the four business owners did the work during that one week. One of the three set up a series of meetings that resulted in more than six figures of projects for his company. The other two got two quick projects just from their initial conversations.

The fourth business owner didn't do the assignment. I asked him, "What got in the way?"

He responded, "I was waiting for it to be perfect."

He didn't do the assignment because he wanted to get the wording right and needed to get "ready" for the conversations. He wanted everything to be "just right." But remember, *he already knew these people*. This was not about making cold calls or doing something ridiculous, or even about spending money. It was a few calls or notes to people who were already friendly with him. Yet he wouldn't do it.

The painfully ironic thing about this story is that the one business owner who didn't do it was the one who needed it the most. His business was in a difficult position, likely because he treated many tasks and projects with that same need to have them perfect first. The others chose to make the calls, and they came away with new revenue. One chose to wait. He chose to "get ready" instead of taking action.

I want you to see from this simple story that waiting to be ready is a *choice*, and to remind you that done and good is better than perfect.

Now look at my experiment through the lens of a test: I offered four people a chance to boost their income, and they all wanted to do it. Three people took action to get quick results—new revenue in only one week. Win or fail, they had their answer to the test, and were ready to go on to testing the next thing that could improve their business. Maybe they could expand their low-hanging fruit lists to include prospects they hadn't talked with in more than a year, or by making calls to business friends who weren't prospects but who might have fresh referrals for them. Or they could improve their processes for following up or pitching new business or retaining current clients. The possibilities for the next test or iteration to run are endless.

## THE TRAP OF SUCCESS

Meanwhile, the other one was...still waiting.

Remember: you can continuously test until you get the desired outcome. In fact, that's exactly the way to proceed.

*"Inaction breeds doubt and fear. Action breeds confidence and courage. If you want to conquer fear, do not sit home and think about it. Go out and get busy."*
—**Dale Carnegie**, Respected Author and Master Influencer

Waiting may seem like a good idea; however, when you look into most situations, you can find actions to take that will help you build momentum and reduce your risks.

Making continuous progress towards anything requires a process of testing and learning. It's a process of constant motion, and it's crucial if you want to grow by actually living life and building your business. Thinking about all of that can be fun, but it doesn't really give you anything. Only *action* will give you feedback on the next steps you should take.

### Testing The Essential

Once you come to understand the essential through a filtering process, you can take action by seeing those essential elements as things to test. And be sure to take action with intensity.

I want to emphasize that both parts are critical: combining the filtering process (finding the essential) and taking action (testing it) is what you must do.

You can't do everything. Even if you are really freaking smart, you still can't do everything. Your ability to change your behavior so that you're doing only the most important things is what will elevate your ability to create a profound shift in the way you get the right work done.

### Focus in an Age of Distraction

We are not hardwired to focus. Worse, we are living in an age of distraction. It takes discipline—intense discipline—to focus on one thing.

When I look back at where I failed to take action in my first business and failed to face my fears, I realized I didn't focus on what was right in front of me. Now, my mission is to serve others to see these essential opportunities and pursue them intently.

 Your job is not to see how to fit in everything you could possibly do. It is to reduce what you do down to the essential.

You might be wondering how this applies to your own journey. It usually shows up in places where you *talk* about doing something but then fail to move forward on it. You might plan, but you don't invest. You might desire a new future, yet you hold yourself back.

You will begin to reverse that trend by finding the essential in every year, every month, and every day. Your job is not to see how to fit in everything you could possibly do. It is to reduce what you do down to the essential.

Then you follow through with action, ideally in an unending series of tests. You develop an understanding of the desired outcome, then devise a way to test it. Get hyper-curious about the results of your testing so that you remove the need for procrastination and perfection.

Test and learn. Test and learn. Keep going until you figure it out.

This is the cycle that allows you to succeed.

The open of this chapter is with a lyric from Elvis Presley about less conversation and more action. Which basically means, less learning and more doing. You create momentum by taking action.

## THE TRAP OF SUCCESS

### Questions to Inspire You

1. What has been your filtering process to determine what is important or essential?
2. What is essential for today? You can pick only one thing.
3. How is procrastination or perfectionism showing up in your life?
4. What is the one thing you will test today to move toward significance?

# 12 THE ROLE OF ADVERSITY

Our biggest problem is that you think you shouldn't have them. Problems make us grow. Problems sculpt our soul.

-Tony Robbins, Business/Life Strategist and Infomercial Giant

## THE TRAP OF SUCCESS

Did you know that Tony Robbins's mother used to beat the crap out of him? Yes, the same Tony Robbins who's known for millions of hours of infomercials and his unmistakable raspy voice. When you meet Robbins, you find out he's beyond tall. He's *huge*. I shook his hand years ago and felt like a child as my hand barely stretched across his palm. Despite his size, his mother did more than anything else to shape who he is, but not in the way mothers traditionally do.

Robbins's childhood was not easy, and in fact it was filled with adversity. He suffered emotionally, not just because he lived in a food-insecure home. He cared for his mother by cooking her meals, and even by convincing the pharmacist to refill medications for her. His mother did love him, and she depended on him. She didn't want him to leave her, so she got physical with him to break his will. For a time, Robbins blamed his mother for their hardships.

As bad as this was for Robbins growing up, he began to realize something that most people won't allow themselves to see: he understood that the adversity in his life shaped him into the man he became. For all that he endured with his mother, he used it to guide the way he loves and serves humanity today. His current view of love came from what he didn't get growing up. His capacity to care came from going without.

Here, Robbins shares how his mother changed his life:

*"If she had been the mother that I wanted, I would not be the man that I am proud to be."*
—**Tony Robbins**, Famed Author and Fire Walker

Without adversity in his life, Robbins would not have had the impact on humanity that he has. Robbins is much more than some self-help guru with perfect teeth. Sure, he continues to do his thing around the world, focused on offering live events like *Unleash the Power Within* and building his many businesses. He continues to coach royalty, heads of state, professional athletes, and celebrities.

But that is not all. Robbins is a millionaire many times over, but he is more attached to significance than to success. His priorities have led him to use his talents and strengths to contribute to the world beyond the traditional measures of success.

His mission—and clearly a deep source of significance for him—is to end hunger for millions of people who are starving. In 2014, Robbins partnered with *Feeding America*, the nation's largest domestic hunger-relief organization, to help provide 100 million meals to families in need. Robbins made a personal commitment of 57 million meals to help inspire even more generosity from others for *Feeding America*, and he builds on that each year by donating proceeds from his latest books and giving more to expand the reach of his mission.

You may not agree with Robbins on everything, or even like him for his personality on TV. But he has become a force to end suffering in this world. And all of it happened because he harnessed the adversity in his life to push himself to serve humanity.

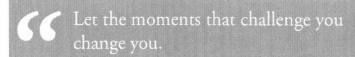

> Let the moments that challenge you change you.

## Adversity Is Not Something to Run Away From

Adversity is part of the journey of living. It's not something to be avoided by living a cautious life. Adversity is what shapes us.

Let your tough times, failures, and adversities add to your character. Let the moments that challenge you change you. As you live your life, embrace the hard experiences that define your thinking. And remember that those times that knock you down are there to make you grow.

Too often, any setback, or even any temporary lack of success, is seen as a failure. But is that really right? When you encounter a barrier, or fail to reach some goal, is all lost?

## THE TRAP OF SUCCESS

What about the benefit of the learning you gained along the way? What about the experience you've added that allows you to do it better the next time? What about the inner growth that comes from dealing with adversity?

Thinking that you must avoid failure at all costs is just one more way that a limited vision of success traps us.

### Examples of Growth Through Adversity

There was once a young man who was cut from his high school basketball team. That moment of failure triggered something inside him. After he dried the tears away, he got to work in earnest on pursuing his dream. That man was Michael Jordan, who hit the NCAA championship-winning shot a few years later, then went on to win six NBA championships, five MVP awards, and 10 scoring titles. Jordan let his moment of adversity propel him to be more.

Or consider the young single mother who finished writing her first novel in cafes while her baby daughter napped beside her. She was jobless, her marriage had ended badly, and for a while she had to rely on government benefits to make ends meet. Her novel was turned down by a dozen publishers before Bloomsbury Publishing bought it...and brought forth *Harry Potter* to the world. Even that debut was inauspicious: just 1,000 copies and an advance of £1,500. But the book began winning awards, then sold for a much higher sum to a U.S. publisher, and soon became a juggernaut worldwide.

No one guaranteed J. K. Rowling that she would succeed, and it took seven turbulent years from the original inspiration for Harry Potter to the publication of the first volume. But Rowling had the kind of grit that allowed her to persevere in the face of adversity.

### Challenging Times Are Opportunities

We have all endured challenging times. They are so much a part of living a worthwhile life that even pointing this out may seem trivial. But I bring it up to get you to look at it differently.

212

When facing a particularly tough phase of life, you can focus on the disappointment. You can worry. You can struggle. But how long do you let yourself wallow in it?

Losing all my money in 2010, losing my business, losing my house, and losing my confidence caused gut-wrenching pain. You have heard this in previous chapters, but I bring it up to help you see that you are not alone. The "2x4 day" that smacked me upside the head knocked me into a pity party for weeks. I laughed a little, but not much. I loved those around me, but not with all of myself. I felt debilitating shame for the pain I had brought to my friends, clients, and most of all my family. There were days when I didn't get out bed. Those dark times caused so much doubt and fear in me. Going through that experience changed me.

In the last seven years, I've talked about this story with thousands of people during interviews, as part of coaching sessions, or after speeches. Over and over again in those settings, I've heard from them about their pain and adversity. For some, it was losing money, or losing someone special in their life. For others, it was having to start over. The common elements were the pain, the loss, and the guilt. For some, there was intense shame.

Take a minute now to think about how you relate to this. What were the most challenging times that caused you to change on the inside?

In my own case, I had to open up to the pain I was feeling before I could stop devoting every waking thought to it. As I began to look toward the future, it was hard at first to see with clarity what I wanted. I remember that one overarching thought for me was that I wanted to make a difference. My life up to that point was about financial success—making the deal, saving money, providing for my family. Yet I was empty inside, with a lack of purpose in what I was doing. As I've told you throughout this book, there was no significance in my work.

As I write this story for you, I am reliving the moments of losing the money and, frankly, experiencing once again that overall feeling of being lost. The shame that I carried with me then was more than I could bear.

I can also remember a recurring thought about significance that kept coming up for me. In the months before, I had been getting treatment from more than a dozen doctors, physical therapists, and chiropractors for an annoying pain in my upper back. It was between my shoulder blades, and likely came from years of sitting hunched over a computer and holding a phone up to my ear with my shoulder.

While in Vancouver (before the "2x4 day"), I started to see a homeopathic professional, Lee Goral. Lee was an angel to me. She tried dozens of different treatments for my pain. I won't rattle them off, but I will say that some embarrassed me and others hurt like hell. I appreciated all that she did for me before the big day. I can tell you that she made a difference in my life. It was about more than taking care of the pain in my back: Lee listened to me and nurtured my soul. I don't remember thanking her properly for this, so this mention in my book will be my expression of gratitude.

I share this part of the story with you because it came back into my mind weeks later, as I was thinking about my next steps. I knew that I would create a new business—I'm an entrepreneur down to my core. I also knew that I didn't want to just chase the money again. I wanted to make a difference.

When I thought of the skills and talent Lee demonstrated in caring for me, I wondered what my own gifts were. Clearly I would not be treating others in a clinic or performing any acts of medical service. But I kept thinking: *How could I make a difference? How could I live with purpose?*

I thought a lot about this in between rounds of working with the attorneys I had hired as the deal was falling apart. Handling the legal side of my business's collapse meant pulling together all my emails and making copies of wire transfer payments. I even sat down with the Secret Service for an interrogation that lasted more than three hours. For the first two hours of that conversation, I had to prove that I was the victim and not the villain. That was *not* fun. After answering all of their questions, it became clear to everyone that I had been squeezed for millions in this deal, and I would have to fight a battle in court to recover the money.

It was exhausting to go back and forth in my mind from the pain of losing it all to how I would keep going forward in life and business. And, given everything else that was going on, I didn't have much free time in my days to figure it out.

One big moment came when I remembered a quote from Maya Angelou. It's the same one I've shared with you more than once already in this book, but it's *that* good:

*"People will forget what you said, people will forget what you did, but people will never forget how you made them feel."*
—**Maya Angelou**, Award-Winning Author and Civil Rights Activist

Those words rang through my head for days. I wanted to make people feel better in some way. I wanted to answer the question, "What will I do to make a difference?"

My answer did not come right away. In fact, it did not come until I started to take action on new ideas. That need for action when you're facing adversity is essential to understand. As you read and complete the exercises I've laid out for you, you are starting to take action. By learning from my adversity and comparing it to your own, you are taking meaningful steps towards meaning and significance. From there, you can start to take more and bigger steps in the direction of your own vision.

## Getting Help in Adversity

I didn't discover what I was going to do over a good cup of coffee, or a through a single session of meditation. I took *action*. Specifically, I had conversations with those around me who could see me without using the lens that I was carrying around with me, which was tinted with failure and loss of confidence. At the same time, I took other practical steps to right the ship of my life and finances as best I could.

In gathering other viewpoints on my situation, I talked to friends who were close to me, and I talked to people who weren't that close to me. I took responsibility for discovering my next steps, and sought out a diversity of views to help improve my thinking.

One conversation I had after the "2x4 day" was with a former coach of mine named Linda Finkle, who had coached me back in 2002 as I was getting my sports tour business off the ground. I introduced you to Linda in Chapter 5 of this book.

One of the biggest benefits of having a coach is being heard. Both when I was starting my sports tour business and after it collapsed, I was able to open up to Linda and talk about the fears that kept me stuck. I still think about those conversations today, and how I had personally changed between 2002 and 2010. Each time, Linda helped me gain more clarity about my business and—more importantly—about myself as a person.

Going back to Linda a few months after losing it all was part of my validation process for becoming a coach myself. I could see what I wanted in the next phase of my life; however, the thought kept playing back in my mind: "Who wants to hire a business coach who just lost millions of dollars?" It is a seemingly "logical" question to ponder, yet it was holding me back from pursuing real significance. Linda's conversation with me helped me see what I could not see on my own. By that point, she had been a coach for more than a decade, and her wisdom was essential for helping me see what was really going on.

She asked me, "Do you think other business owners have endured similar setbacks and losses in their entrepreneurial journeys?"

216

You know the answer to that question as well as I did. Of course they have. Far from alienating me from business owners, my huge setback would help me to understand them—and help them to know that I really did grasp their challenges and fears. Talking with Linda helped me to see how what happened to me could be used to relate to others in their businesses.

At the same time that my conversations with Linda and others inspired me toward a new vision of my life and work, I had to take many practical—and humbling—steps to deal with the aftermath of losing all my money. My wife and I had to drastically cut expenses to survive. We moved from our big house to a rental, and sold off furniture and even toys. I had no business and no income, yet had to stay busy with the cleanup from losing it all. Life was changing fast, yet at the time making any progress at all felt agonizingly slow.

My search for meaning in life and ways to make a difference was a process. My drive to seek significance started with the adversity of losing it all. I'm not comparing my success to becoming the greatest basketball player of all time—or, for that matter, comparing getting cut from the varsity as a high school sophomore to losing your livelihood as a grown man. But my trajectory was a little like Michael Jordan's: the setback became a starting point for pursuing something bigger. The adversity was a catalyst to where I was supposed to be.

I pulled at that thread to see where it would take me. I took action, starting with deep conversations about myself and how I could make an impact. I took that quote from Maya Angelou to heart and focused on how I could make others feel through my work.

The cover-up prevents us from really learning the lesson we need to learn from the adversity.

## THE TRAP OF SUCCESS

My adversity presented an opportunity that I had ignored for years. You see it, right? The pain and struggle of losing it all became necessary for me to change how I saw life.

### The Lesson of Adversity

You do some of your best work when challenges and hard times force you to do more with less. You have to look inside yourself to find out the real truth. You have to pull back the layers of stories and B.S. (i.e., "Belief System"). You pull all of that away to get to the core issue: the underlying beliefs that have shaped your adversity.

There is one thing that gets in the way—what I call the cover-up. I have seen it over and over: people become masters at covering up their pain or adversity. They push all of it down and put smiles on their faces to show the world. You see this all the time on Facebook (or, as I sometimes call it, Fakebook). We share the best versions of our lives to show others how good we have it. I've done it. Likely you have, too. The cover-up prevents us from really learning the lesson we need to learn from the adversity.

I have noticed that when people stop covering up and become vulnerable about the adversity they have faced, they open up to the world and connect with others in a deeper way. I could write for pages on this one topic, giving you story after story about people I've coached. Instead, I invite you to explore this idea for yourself. Share your own lessons. Share your own pain. Share them with others who will appreciate who you are because of what you have endured.

I love the way that Brené Brown, Ph.D., author of *Rising Strong: The Reckoning, The Rumble, The Revolution*, talks about vulnerability. Brown made her mark with a 2010 TEDx talk called "The Power of Vulnerability" that is one of the top five most-viewed TED talks of all time, with tens of millions of views.

Brown has researched the topics of vulnerability and shame at a deeper level than anyone; her viewpoints are grounded in years of social

218

research into the lives of those who have navigated adversity. She asks the question: *Where in our lives did vulnerability become a weakness?* In her years of studying this subject, she has found that vulnerability is essential to our growth and connection with others. To put it bluntly, vulnerability is a strength.

Brown's work shows the need for vulnerability in our lives, and it links happiness and the feeling of belonging with our core identity. She knows that you have to bring all of you to life and resist the need to numb yourself, whether it's with alcohol, drugs, shopping, or cupcakes.

*"We can't be all in, if only part of us shows up."*
—**Brené Brown**, Researcher-Storyteller, and Shame Expert

In Brown's book *Rising Strong*, I was surprised and thrilled to see a friend of mine appear when she talks about trust. Charles Feltman (introduced to you in Chapter 3), author of *The Thin Book of Trust*, describes trust as "choosing to risk making something you value vulnerable to another person's actions." Charles was one of my instructors during my certification to be a coach. He helped me through my need for forgiveness—specifically by helping me discover that what I really sought was how to forgive myself.

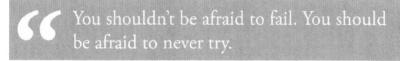

" You shouldn't be afraid to fail. You should be afraid to never try.

### It Is All in Your Perspective

Failure is neither good or bad. It just is. Failure at attaining some goal is part of the journey. However, most people have one or two perspectives on failure that get in the way of their growth.

One of those perspectives is "You must avoid failure." This one appeals to the risk-averse people who would rather risk nothing so they can avoid the pain of failure. These people avoid putting themselves out there. So even if they want more from life and business, they let their mindset of fear keep them from trying.

## THE TRAP OF SUCCESS

I personally believe you shouldn't be afraid to fail. You should be afraid to never try. I live by this motto now, after all I have been through.

The second limiting perspective is, "Failure is not an option." We talked about this one back in Chapter 3, when I was going over my (false) "truths" I had to let go of so I could see *the* truth and grow as a person. This belief that failure is not an option keeps a lot of people pushing hard and driving toward an end goal. This is a common perspective shared by many entrepreneurs, Type A people, and others that causes them to miss the lessons of failure.

When you believe that failure is a bad thing, you avoid big goals, if you're risk-averse, or else you grind yourself down, if you're driven. Either way, you will struggle to learn the lessons that failure is trying to teach you. You might even have to repeat those same lessons over and over again. I know I'm not alone in this.

### Shifting Your View of Failure

One visionary leader has built a billion-dollar brand by understanding failure and having a different perspective on it than most people do. You may have heard about Sara Blakely, who single-handedly created a new segment of undergarments for women (and a few brave men) to manage their bulges under their clothes.

Blakely is the founder and CEO of Spanx. With no business experience or even business classes in school, Sara had the bright idea to invent a new product that no one said they wanted. Spanx started as a product for women to hold in the bulges that are caused with traditional girdles and to smooth out panty lines under their clothes. They became a hit with millions of women across America who wanted to look their best. Celebrities started to talk about the powers of Spanx in interviews. The "movement" of Spanx took off.

Blakely didn't have it easy to bring her product to market. For months, she tried to get the attention of women's hosiery companies for a product that sounded odd to them. She didn't let that stop her. She made dozens of in-person meetings to the mills and got the brush-off there, too. That didn't stop her, either, and today Spanx has hundreds of millions of dollars in annual revenue. Blakely herself is a billionaire. The end of the story for Blakely and Spanx has yet to be written, but the story's beginning exemplifies how adversity becomes opportunity.

Are you wondering what made Blakely push through all that adversity in building her company? Are you curious about what makes her see things differently from most people?

The first time I heard her story, I thought about her ability to handle failure and keep going, her courage to innovate, and all the no's she heard along the way. It would have been so easy for her to stop. Then recently I saw her speak about how she was taught to handle failure growing up.

Blakely's father would encourage failure in their home. At the dinner table, Blakely and her brother would be quizzed by their father about the "failures of the week." If Sara tried something and failed, he would give her a high five. He saw the value in—and encouraged—*trying*. That is quite different from most upbringings, but her father had a core belief that growth comes through failure.

That experience with her father allowed her to see failure differently than most people. She said:

*"Failure for me became not trying versus the outcome. So many people don't take risks for the fear of failure. They don't start the business, they don't go create the art they want to create, or they don't go try out to be in the play, or whatever it is, for the fear of failure."*
—**Sara Blakely,** Billionaire Entrepreneur and Failure Specialist

Reframing failure is the key. Blakely believes that failure comes in *not trying*. In addition to reframing failure, she would look for the hidden gifts of those moments. She calls them the "amazing nuggets." These are the lessons that you would not want to give up.

221

## THE TRAP OF SUCCESS

You have probably heard about similar concepts, like looking for the silver lining. But are you applying it? Are you living your life by looking for areas where you can expand through failure? If you are doing this now, how can you take it deeper? How can you catch it sooner? How can you become more aware of the gifts provided through adversity?

### The Meaning We Assign to Failure

It is not our failures that define us. It is how we interpret them. The bigger part of the journey is what you do *after* you fail—who you become, what beliefs you hold on to.

My loss of millions does not define me. It is only one part of my journey. The biggest part, though, is what I decided to do next—the person I decided to become.

Don't just take my word for it. Another guest on the podcast was Ryan Estis, a phenomenal professional speaker on topics of leadership and change. Ryan's worldview agrees that life is not about the hard times. It is about the meaning we assign to those moments.

Ryan has faced adversity and overcome challenges in his own life. And for the last 15 years, he has been working with companies and their leaders to shift the way they work and lead. During our interview, we talked about the value of being uncomfortable and letting that discomfort change you. You'll hear the echoes of how I opened this section of the chapter:

*"It is not the failures that define us. There is a benefit of adversity...the ups, downs, and sideways parts of life. It is how we interpret those moments that shape our lives."*
—**Ryan Estis,** Master Marketer and Superstar Speaker

What meaning are you assigning to your failures? Do you have the courage to accept the truths that are revealed in those moments?

## One True Activator

One of the most powerful ways to keep yourself open to those lessons, continue growing, and handle any disappointments along the way is to focus on gratitude. Gratitude is an idea that's tossed around so much that it has become something we take for granted, which is tragically ironic.

Gratitude is not just a word. It is a genuinely deep realization that you appreciate something that has come to you out of grace. Many people confuse this with saying "thank you." But the phrase "thank you" is what you say in response to someone giving you something or doing something for you.

"Thank you" becomes the response for that gift. But gratitude comes when you were not given something. For example, if it has been raining for days and you walk outside to feel the sun peeking through clouds. The rain stops. You wouldn't say "thank you," would you? You would have gratitude for that moment of sunshine breaking through to your skin.

That is the feeling you need to focus on when things are going against you. If you're open to it, gratitude becomes the activator for your next steps even in the midst of your worst adversity.

Think about that feeling of gratitude for the sunshine on your skin—so simple, but so pure and good—acting as a counterweight to the failure and pain. If you can't find something to be grateful for in your adversity, then you aren't looking hard enough. Life's failures always include something to be grateful for—the silver lining, the "amazing nuggets."

Besides, if you can't be grateful for what you already have, what makes you think there will be joy in getting what you are working for now?

Gratitude is a powerful way to break free from frustration. You can't be grateful and frustrated at the same time. It's not how the brain works.

## THE TRAP OF SUCCESS

One key exercise to activate gratitude is to follow this three-step plan:

1. Take a moment to step back (literally or in your mind) from the moment you're experiencing.
2. Look for even the smallest part of it that you can appreciate.
3. Express gratitude to someone for what you feel.

Don't forget the third step. Don't forget to express your gratitude to others.

*"Unexpressed gratitude feels like ingratitude to the ones for whom you are grateful."*
—**Andy Stanley**, Eloquent Pastor and Powerful Catalyst

I'll be brutally candid: there will be good days and bad days ahead of you. That's the blessing and the challenge of being an entrepreneur or an employee. Actually, it's called being human! But in every adversity, there is the seed of equal or greater benefit...**if** you will allow yourself to see it.

Years ago, I was watching the movie "Soul Surfer," which is about Bethany Hamilton's bounceback from a shark attack to become a pro surfer. When asked, "Would you go back to that day of the shark attack and decide not to surf?" Bethany says that should would not change a thing. As she puts it, she will reach more people with one arm than two.

The same goes for me. I suffered through the betrayal of the "2x4 day," but since then I am becoming stronger than ever. I am connected to a higher purpose of serving others.

I am grateful for what happened to me. I see it is as a gift that has allowed me to find significance in life, both personal and professional. And I realize it is all due to how I choose to interpret my adversity.

### From Adversity to Transformation
The moments in life that cause the most pain will also be the most

224

transformational. And the people who walk that journey with you will be lifelong friends. Your adversity creates perspective in your life. It will allow you to handle setbacks, endure criticism, and never give up on your quest for significance.

Dealing with life's adversity requires expressing vulnerability, reframing the meaning of failure, and finding the gratitude in those moments.

In the next chapter, we will take one last look at the journey to significance.

## Questions to Inspire You

1. What key lessons have you learned through adversity in your life?
2. Looking back, what are you most grateful for now?
3. How can you embrace failure in a new way to support your personal growth?

# 13

## THE JOURNEY OF SIGNIFICANCE

We see the world, not as it is, but as we are.

-Stephen Covey, Applauded Author and Remarkable Speaker

CHAPTER THIRTEEN

## THE TRAP OF SUCCESS

You will receive in life who you become. Period.

You change the world when you change yourself; that is how it works.

To create significance for others, you have to become significant to yourself.

You cannot create a life of significance—one in which you contribute to others—until you first become a person who can accept that significance.

That journey to creating a new way of living and seeing the world is unpredictable and full of discovery. It will be hampered by homeostasis, our natural drive to keep things the same as they have always been. That natural inclination to resist change will try to keep you right where you are, even if it is no good for you.

Making anything stick takes commitment and discipline. But it doesn't stop there. You need to have the right strategy, develop the right practices, and stay persistent. The journey of significance is filled with challenges to overcome and doubt to surmount. Yet significance is the dream that makes living and working worth it.

When I talk about "significance" here, I'm including the whole project of pushing your boundaries, escaping your comfort zone, and reimagining your life and work to achieve both significance for others and new, exponential levels of success on your own terms. Transcending success as most define it—the trap we've been talking about throughout this book—will test you and provoke resistance, from your own subconscious and from some of the people in your life who can't imagine you as more than you are today. You are going beyond the limits of ordinary experience to create work that excites you, work that is purpose-driven, and that's going to unsettle some people, including yourself. But following that path will cause you to grow and expand who you are.

Now you face a choice: to continue on your current path or to take this new path toward fulfillment. Because you've made it this far in the book, I assume you're ready for that new way of being.

## Your Gifts

It is my belief that each person on the earth has gifts. That means *you* have gifts.

Discovering your gifts can only occur through real experience. You can't just sit and think about them in the abstract; you have to tie them back to things you've actually done. So reflect on your experience and start making a list to answer this question: *What comes easily to you?* It might be hard to see sometimes, because it is easy to take your own gifts for granted. You may have a limited view on this because you think that everyone has the same abilities, or that it's "no big deal" to do the things that come easily to you. Yet it's a trap to think that what is easy for you is also easy for others.

You have a responsibility to develop your particular gifts. Just because something is natural to you does not mean you can expect those gifts to grow on their own. It is like the gifted natural athlete who expects to go straight into the pros and excel. That raw talent must be used and shaped and challenged into real ability that's backed by skill. And I will say this, too: you must have someone outside yourself to guide you to greatness. Every professional athlete has a coach. Not some of them. Not most of them. *Every one* of them. They know the value of having someone analyze and challenge their performance and their thinking to encourage their growth and help them get to the next level.

You must also show your gifts to the world so that others can see your value. I see so many people who think that just having a gift is enough. They are waiting to be discovered instead of hustling to share their gifts with the world, and many of them will be waiting forever.

## Leading Leaders

My mission is to get you (and millions of others) to have the courage to share your gifts with the people you are here to serve. For some of you, your gift will be the creation of a new technology or service. For others, it will be your ability to transform others and help bring their gifts into the world. This is going to be a big part of your journey if you see yourself as a leader. Leaders develop other leaders.

Leading others is part of the process. When you use what you have in the betterment of others, you also change. When they feel your care, they grow— but *you* grow, too. This is a crucial part of the journey to significance.

When you choose that journey, it is not a selfish choice, because you are committing to giving to others with your time, money, and gifts. You will be expanding their view of the world.

### Being the Gift
Some of you will even step up to be a gift to all of humanity. I first heard this concept of "being the gift" from a friend of mine, Shannon Graham. Shannon shared with me his views of deep transformation during some amazing conversations on the podcast.

Knowing your gifts and serving others is just the start. Some people like Gandhi and Mother Teresa end up giving themselves to the world. How far you take your gift is about who you are at the very core of your being. It is about BEING a gift to those around you. Warning: this requires deeper thinking than just showing up. You have to truly grapple with your whole concept of how you give of yourself to others.

If this is your path, you will hear it calling to you. It will start as a whisper and grow louder and louder as you get past the *longing* for significance and begin to really *do something* about it. You will be challenged, and you will likely resist it. Conventional thinking will steer you away from the challenge, but I can tell you from experience that ignoring that call will cause you pain. I believe this is what happened with me when I lost it all. I felt the need to do more for humanity besides just make money. I wanted it, yet at first I was not willing to shift my thinking to accept it.

230

*"When people do not expand, or place conditions on themselves to stop their expansion, that is when they experience the most pain."*
—**Shannon Graham**, Master Coach and Guide to Visionary Leaders

## No Settling
You don't have to settle. You don't have to tolerate your current life or level of success. Even if things are good now, you can make them outstanding. Escaping the trap of success is about breaking free from the comfort of what you have always done. It is about getting uncomfortable with yourself so you can have something new and better.

You can be grateful for what you have and still want to create more. You just have to be willing to expand into that new area. You have to envision the path. You have to create new strategies. You have to do the work.

Settling is easy, and it easily becomes a pattern. Choosing to create significance is hard, and it will strike you at your core. You will feel the effort, and it won't feel comfortable. That's a good thing.

Before we jump into the final steps to significance, consider this...we fulfill ourselves in growing our mind, bodies, and spirits by contributing to others. You can't achieve real fulfillment purely for selfish reasons. You have to accept that significance comes with a need to impact others. That requires change.

And being an agent of change for others means also accepting change inside of yourself.

## How Are You Showing Up?
Odd question, I know. When I ask groups, "How are you showing up?" I get lots of answers.

What I mean by this question is how clear people are regarding who you are and what you're all about based on how you appear and act and move through the world. How intentional are you about your emotions? How confident are you about *you*?

231

It's not specifically about your clothes or your hair—I'm not getting into fashion tips here—though if you want to influence others you do need to be aware and intentional about the external impression you make so that you can reach people.

Your answer to the question "How are you showing up?" is important. Having that awareness and intentionality about every external aspect of your demeanor—your body language, your tone of voice, your attitude, the words you use, how you project yourself in the world—is crucial for your journey to significance.

Now I'll walk you through seven areas that are essential to how you are showing up. Several of these will echo what you've read in prior chapters, but I want to bring them all together here so that you can see how they fit together in sequence as you follow the path toward significance and new levels of success.

### Step 1: Mission

This goes back to what we discussed in Chapter 5. When you have a mission that is bigger than you, you see the world differently. You develop the ability to go beyond your personal needs. Fulfillment becomes less about your net worth and more about your impact for others.

As touched on in previous chapters, I commonly encounter some level of bargaining when I mention the need for a personal mission. People get especially sensitive when it comes to providing for their families, and I certainly understand that from my own experience. Yet the "mission" you are on for real fulfillment is likely to go beyond serving only your family. It expands to include some bigger slice of humanity.

Your mission clearly defines *who* you are serving and *what* you do for them. It is simple and inspiring.

*Check out the free companion exercises on my site for more examples and a special training that helps you create your mission. http:// thetrapofsuccess.com/companion-exercises*

A powerful mission has clarity and inspires you to create a different world than is visible today. As we first discussed in Chapter 5, that new view of the future is called your vision.

## Step 2: Vision

How clearly can you see the future for yourself? Is it fuzzy? Is in incomplete? I've talked with thousands of people about creating a new vision, which has only strengthened my belief that you can't wait for life to happen to you. You must define the life you want, and then work hard to change and grow to be the person who can receive that life. The destination or future you're working for is your vision.

When your vision is clear and compelling, it will pull you forward. Let me stress the "pull" here. You don't want your vision to *push* you toward something. You want it to be so vivid that you are pulled to create the new future. You are pulled to transform your whole being in service of the vision.

A vision does not require you to know how to do it. The "how" comes after you decide where you are going. Now, to make your vision come alive, you will need to define your values.

## Step 3: Aligned Values

Values are more than words hanging on the walls of your company. They are guideposts to what is important to you or the organization. Most businesses don't have clear values, or, if they do, there are too many of them to do much good.

But the real issue is that most companies don't align their leadership to their values. This means that the daily decisions of the business, big and small, are not filtered through the values of the company by those who run the company.

I help people discover their values in my work. This means getting to a core set of words that genuinely reflect their most important beliefs, and that in turn shape how they operate.

233

## THE TRAP OF SUCCESS

The word "aligned" here is about who you truly are in your essence. It is not about doing what you are "supposed to" do. Or "should" do. It is about the spirit inside you. When your actions are aligned with your values, you are living your truest self.

One way to clarify your mission, vision, and values is to write your own Manifesto. Your manifesto puts into words each of these elements that pull you forward. Here is my manifesto: http://leadersinthetrenches. com/manifesto/

*Check out the free companion exercises on my site for more examples and a special training that helps you define your values. http:// thetrapofsuccess.com/companion-exercises*

I also believe that you must love what you are doing for your work to be aligned with your mission and vision. If you are settling for where you are now, it will be hard for you to be fulfilled. That doesn't mean you will love all parts of what you do. For example, as a speaker, I have to travel a lot. Travel is hard on the body (crappy food choices, uncomfortable beds, time zone changes...) and it is hard on family life. But I do it because I love connecting with audiences and helping them along their own paths to significance, so even the lousy parts of the job are tolerable because I know that they are a minor price to pay for loving what I do and being aligned with my values in the bigger picture. And in that bigger picture, if you don't have love for what you are doing, you'll never feel the sense of significance in your work.

Part of loving what you do is having a good attitude about it. Your thoughts shape everything in your life—every action you take, every commitment, and every relationship. So let's talk about the inner game.

### Step 4: The Inner Game — Mindset Matters Most
Think back on what we discussed in Chapter 10 about "playing to win," and especially how our mindsets impact that. You operate every day with 50,000 - 70,000 thoughts in your head. Most of them are pre-programmed by the beliefs you carry around, which shape every

decision you make and action you take. Your mind controls it all. You can wish for things to be different. But if your mindset won't allow you to conceive of the new thoughts, attitudes and actions you will need to take, you won't ever do what you must to achieve your vision.

I want you to remember a quotation that will simplify this concept for you—the same one I used at the start of this chapter. It has helped me grow as a leader, entrepreneur, husband, and father:

*"We see the world, not as it is, but as we are."*
—**Stephen Covey,** Author and Thought Leader

This is a deep piece of wisdom that has resonated across many cultures, religions, and philosophies. What it boils down to is that two people can encounter the same thing and experience it very differently based on their own mindset, experiences, and point of view. Let's take a trivially simple example and say that you and I are each given identical slices of pizza when we're hungry. I say to myself, "Sausage and pepperoni—my favorite!" and start to salivate; but you look at it and think about how much you dislike pepperoni (or cheese, or tomato sauce), or maybe you're a vegetarian and would never eat sausage, and you're repulsed. Same pizza, wildly different reactions.

Now take this deeper into your own thinking. If you believe something is impossible, you will likely not even attempt it. Now, we could probably think of exceptions to this, but it's the most common way of operating in our world.

When it comes to achieving your vision and the journey to significance, your mindset matters most. The thinking patterns you cultivate *become* your reality. When you are faced with moments of opportunity, you will make the choice to accept or resist them based on your thinking—your perception of reality.

Your perceptions, your thoughts, your mindset—*these* are the things that will affect how intently you focus on your vision. How you handle distractions. How you make decisions. The courage you show. Your level of persistence.

You can use the "Courage List" I described in Chapter 9 to help you on your way, along with the other exercises throughout this book and on my website. But whatever you do, you must master the inner game so that you can be comfortable with being uncomfortable, and so you can play to win. Don't look for an "easy button," because there are no shortcuts.

Your mindset shapes each and every step of your journey, and it flows into the strategies that you will explore and choose for yourself.

### Step 5: The Right Strategy

Look at your options—*all* of them, not just the ones you're comfortable with. Remember that you always have a choice. It is *always* there if you allow yourself to see it.

I'm a business strategist, which means I help companies, leaders, and entrepreneurs find new strategies for attaining their goals. Really, that's another way of saying that I help them turn their visions into reality. The challenging part for me is never about coming up with the strategies (that's my gift), but always about getting my clients to consider strategies they don't believe will work for them. The specific resistance may arise from fear of doing something like speaking in public, or uncertainty about a new approach to sales or marketing, but in the end it always comes back to expanding their view of themselves and what is *possible*.

Part of my success today comes in getting clients to look at the truth of what's working and what's not, and then to let go of the strategies that have distracted them from their goals, or that worked in the past but aren't producing results anymore.

On this point, recall the story of Ron Dod in Chapter 10: his company exploded in revenue (remember: *412 percent growth in 12 months*), but

236

only after he let go of the services and clients that no longer fit with his vision, then adopted new strategies that weren't even on his radar before. Ron's courage to change strategies made all the difference.

I remind you of Ron's story to help you look beyond what you have done in the past. Let go of the old ways. Allow new results to happen by embracing new strategies.

*Check out the free companion exercises on my site for more examples and a special training that helps you define your strategies. http:// thetrapofsuccess.com/companion-exercises*

## Step 6: Action
We can see sharp distinctions among those who aren't successful, those who are trapped in a limited view of success, and those who have broken through to exponential success. It is even more rare to find people who have joined that last category while also having a true feeling of significance.

What sets them apart? Over the past 5 years, I have interviewed and coached hundreds of people, spoken to thousands more, and studied the traits of the ultra-successful very, very closely. One of the simplest, yet most profound, differences that I have observed is that those who achieve more are **action takers**. Action is part of their *being*.

This isn't about hustling all the time. You path might be different than other people's in that regard. But you still must be willing to take action on your dreams. Being an action taker is about seeing opportunities to expand your reach—to expand yourself—and then seizing those opportunities through what you *do*.

Action takers typically do most or all of the following:
- Decide quickly if an option drives them toward their goals or is merely a distraction
- Create a plan of action
- Study the success of those ahead of them

## THE TRAP OF SUCCESS

- Muster the courage to take the first real step toward something new, then the next and the next
- Move forward despite any fears
- Avoid the doubts that would arise if they asked "What if it doesn't work for me?" or "What will they think of me?"—by not subjecting themselves to those derailing questions in the first place
- Focus on the most important aspects without getting hung up on the fine details that probably don't matter
- Banish the need for perfection (which is a great enemy of achievement)

Those who take it to the next level are the people who do these things with persistence, resilience, and tenacity. They don't look for excuses for why something isn't working—they focus on how to make it work for them, or on what would work better instead. They are also not quick to jump from one strategy to another midstream, or to be seduced by the newest "shiny object" that comes along, either.

And here comes the **knockout punch**: even if you are already an action taker, what is required to get more from your current actions?

Ready?

### Focus

Many people struggle with focus. Sometimes the core issue is procrastination. Other times it's a struggle to avoid being distracted by trivial things. Often it comes because they haven't done the work to clarify their mission, vision, values, and strategies. (See how it all links up?)

A simple example: when my son was four years old, he and I had an experience that underlined the importance of focus for me. My son received a jigsaw puzzle for Christmas that was more difficult than he could handle. It was too challenging for his attention span, and almost too much for mine. Just keeping it real here.

First we had to reduce outside distractions, for example by turning off the TV. I wasn't used to doing puzzles and didn't have any fancy strategies beyond starting at the outer edges and working my way in. But after more than an hour of work, we hadn't made much progress.

I ramped up my intensity just so we could finish the puzzle before my son's bedtime. I focused intently on one small element of the puzzle so I could match up even a few pieces. For example, I would look for a spot of color not found elsewhere in the puzzle so I could locate that one piece.

As I continued with this strategy, I began to pick up momentum. New pieces started clicking into place faster, and finally we finished—before bedtime. It was a great, simple exercise in focus, and it reminded me that, in order to solve some of our key issues in life, we need to learn to concentrate at a new level.

Even with all the work I've done on this over the years, I am continuing to train myself to focus on my priorities—the essential few things—on command, and continuing to reap the rewards of that. I want to challenge you to look for new ways to bring greater focus and concentration to your mission, your vision, your values. Change the patterns and habits underlying your thoughts and behaviors, and you will find new ways to concentrate on what's important. That higher level of focus, in turn, will help you pursue your vision and expand your boundaries better than ever.

*Check out the free resources on my website for companion exercises, more examples, and a special training that helps you improve your focus in service of the journey of significance. http://thetrapofsuccess.com/ companion-exercises*

## Step 7: Results
Significance comes from real impact. That means achieving *results*. You have to have some idea of the intended results of your actions—who will be affected, what will change—to have a feeling of significance. In

my experience, this is more about direction and momentum than it is about specific goals.

We all know that, in the absence of results, we are spinning our wheels. But to get the right results, you need to tie your quest for results to all the steps before this one.

It starts with mission and vision. If you lack clarity about these—about your direction in life—you won't have a personally meaningful standard to measure yourself against. Without that, you'll remain stuck in the trap of measuring success by your bank account, your possessions, your job title, or some other ultimately trivial standard.

Once you clearly understand your mission and vision, your standard of measurement will be quite different. And it will come down to the impact you have on others.

Your results must also align with your values. If you are not intentional about clarifying and honoring your values, you could achieve all of your goals, yet still have that aching feeling of "Is this it?" As you know by now, I experienced years of that back when I didn't have any clear idea of applying my values to my life and business.

Only you can feel the results that flow from a life of significance. You sense them with your heart. You feel them in your level of confidence. In short, you will come to measure results on your own terms, not anyone else's.

### Who Are You BEING?
I often ask my clients, "Who do you need to BE to have the success you want?" The key word here is "BE."

Who are you *being* right now? How does that way of *being* limit your success and your significance?

This book has looked at success and significance from many

240

perspectives. I've put a spotlight on the various ways we get trapped by success so that you can understand what might be holding you back. I hope that by now you are developing a keen awareness of what you want and how you need to shift your mindset and your actions to accept it and make it happen in your life.

My aim is for you to be willing to shift from the inside out, for you to see the inner battles that keep you playing small and staying comfortable, and then to master the inner game, which will free you up so you can operate boldly even when you're uncomfortable. When you get real and look into the mirror, you can now be honest with yourself about who you are currently *being* in this world, and how that person has kept you from finding the joy in significance.

## Who Do You Need to BE?

The big question that follows is obvious: Who do you need to *be* to attain *significance?*

This isn't about what you will feel in a single moment in time. I'm talking about creating a lifetime that is filled with the feeling of significance. As you take the journey of significance I've explained here, you will feel it more and more.

To be "ambitious" is not enough. To be "motivated" is not enough. To dedicate every breath in your body to achieving significance—that's the path I'm pointing you to.

Passion is critical, because the journey is hard. You will be required to do what others will not do. You will face adversity that will make you want to stop, but that's when you will dig deeper, learn new lessons, and find new resources inside yourself.

Your breakthrough will come from the habits that build significance. They will emerge over time as you apply the lessons in this book. You will more quickly see the gifts that come with every failure. You will think bigger—not because somebody said you should, but because your vision commands you to. At that point, you will become endlessly proactive about creating what you want, no longer waiting for it to develop without your input.

When you reach that state, you will *automatically* look for the edges of your comfort zone. You'll embrace your uneasiness as a signal showing you where you need to grow. You'll lean into your fears and open yourself up to the courage that will guide you on your journey. You will play to win instead of playing not to lose. You will insist on doing only what is essential, and perform endless tests to find out what works best. You will thrive on taking new actions and getting new results.

Isn't that the life you really want?

Remember that you can only control who **you** are being in this world. You can't control others. You can't control results. But you do get to choose how you show up in the world, how you interpret life, and how you respond to what happens.

Escaping the trap of success and making the shift to exponential success and significance will come from your new ability to see the choices you have and select the ones that connect to your mission, your vision, your values—and ultimately your soul.

Will you stay trapped where you are? Or choose to join the dance of significance and exponential success?

# ESCAPING THE TRAP OF SUCCESS AT ANY SCALE: CORPORATION, BUSINESS UNIT, CIVIC GROUP, CHURCH, OR TEAM

You can't leave yet. I'm not done. I'm going to leave you with this final thought.

*The Trap of Success* shares examples and stories from my view of entrepreneurial growth, but it doesn't stop there.

Don't you dare think this is just about you and your professional life. It is about so much more. This book is meant to activate you so that you can carry your mission out into all parts of the world. This means the small groups as well as the larger ones, too.

There is a UNIVERSAL message in this book that applies to all organizations and entities regardless of their scale:

- Corporations and their parts: business units, departments, teams
- Non-profits
- Governments
- Churches
- Sports Teams
- Civic Groups
- Communities

...and any other organization that has been caught in the drift of its current level of success.

243

## THE TRAP OF SUCCESS

Think about the groups that you are involved with right now. It can be the company where you work, or another organization you support. Here is a simple exercise to guide your thinking and help you *take action* in service of those organizations.

**List your top 2 or 3 organizations on a piece of paper by name.**

Use the questions that follow to assess where each organization stands right now, rating it with a number from 1 to 10. If the organization has reached full potential for a question, give them a 10. If it is in severe need of a new approach, give them a 1.

Assess each organization with the following questions:

**Has this organization reached its full potential of significance?** This addresses the contribution it makes to those outside the organization. (No 10's allowed on this one, as there is always room for growth.)

**Does the organization have a clear mission and vision that is known by everyone in it?**

**Does the organization have a consistent mode of operation that you would consider proactive?**

**Does the organization seek areas that are uncomfortable so that it and the people within it can continue to grow?**

**Does the organization lead with courage, internally and externally?**

**Does the organization play to win when it comes to its impact on others?**

These questions are BIG and BOLD, yet the insights you gain from doing this exercise will guide you to the areas of opportunity where you can step in and expand your significance beyond your own personal goals. If one of the organizations you care about—your employer, your church, your kids' school—is lacking in one of these areas, accept

244

the challenge to alter its course toward significance and breakthrough success.

You are here for a reason. You chose to read THIS book for a reason. You are not satisfied with the old way of chasing incremental success. You are not satisfied with limited thinking, neglected relationships, and an unrealized need for fulfillment. And you are not going to wait until "someday," after you've achieved your personal success, to make a bigger impact and achieve significance.

## Creating Significance at a Larger Scale

We all want different things, and each person reading this book will have a different measure of significance. The differences among us are one of the factors that make life so interesting—and sometimes frustrating, too. But don't give up: whether you're finding significance at a personal level or bringing greater significance to a whole organization, the journey is worth it.

This book is here to guide you and help you see what lies ahead on that journey. The path will not be easy...but it is not supposed to be. Using the answers to the exercise above, consider how each of the organizations in your life can benefit from a clear understanding of how significance is created, and how significance can dance with exponential success.

You are a catalyst for every person and every group around you. Don't let reading this book be simply a moment in time. Let it change you and how you interact with all of the organizations in your life.

The impact you have—and the significance you create—is up to you.

## THE TRAP OF SUCCESS

Congratulations for reading the whole book. It is an honor to serve you. I have written three case studies that will give you insights about significance that you can access in the SECRET CHAPTER.

1) **Adam Walker and Jeff Hilimire** — How did they create 48 non-profit websites in 48 hours at no cost to the non-profits? Let me share with you the story of how they used their talents to create a movement that is spreading around the world.

2) **Stefanie Diaz** — How did she change her business model to serve the right people? Stefanie's story is remarkable in that she is not only affecting her clients, but also creating a huge change within her own confidence.

3) **Tom's Shoes** — How can a company impact the world through their business? See inside the journey of a company that has seen how significance and success dance together.

Get the SECRET CHAPTER: The Case Studies by going to http://thetrapofsuccess.com/secret

# Resources

**Introduction**

- **Success Magazine:** This initial story was written by me (Gene Hammett) and originally published for Success Magazine on March 31, 2016 and has been modified for the book: http://www.success.com/blog/how-i-lost-3-million-in-24-hours-and-bounced-back
- **James Moriarty** - My attorney http://www.moriarty.com/
- **Filippo Marchino and Damon Rogers** - My attorneys http://www.thexlawgroup.com/
- **Maya Angelou** - https://www.mayaangelou.com/
- **Leaders in the Trenches** - My podcast http://leadersinthetrenches.com

**Chapter 1**

- **NetVendor** - A provider of business-to-business (B2B) e-commerce consulting services https://www.crunchbase.com/organization/netvendor-2
- **Tony Robbins** - Feeding America http://www.feedingamerica.org/hunger-in-america/news-and-updates/press-room/press-releases/tony-robbins-provides-Millions-Meals.html

**Chapter 2**

- **Rich Litvin:** http://leadersinthetrenches.com/164 (podcast interview)
- **Martin Luther King:** http://www.huffingtonpost.com/2013/01/21/oprahs-favorite-mlk-quote_n_2496816.html
- **Sam Polk:** https://www.nytimes.com/2014/01/19/opinion/sunday/for-the-love-of-money.html

**Chapter 3**

- **Ryan Estis:** http://leadersinthetrenches.com/210 (podcast interview)
- **Charles Feltman:** Insight Coaching https://insightcoaching.com/business-coaching/

## RESOURCES

- **Adam Braun:** The Promise of a Pencil: How an Ordinary Person Can Create Extraordinary Change http://amzn.to/2gP62FG
- **Rich Litvin:** http://leadersinthetrenches.com/164 (podcast interview)
- **Mike Pisciotta:** http://leadersinthetrenches.com/234 (podcast interview) and http://www.marketingyourpurpose.com/ex-con-started-nothing-build-7-figure-business/

### Chapter 4

- **Sean Stephens:** http://leadersinthetrenches.com/224; Get Off Your "But": How to End Self-Sabotage and Stand Up for Yourself http://amzn.to/2vNTsxr
- **Dan Sullivan:** http://leadersinthetrenches.com/208 (podcast interview); The Dan Sullivan Question http://amzn.to/2vOUMzM
- **Henry Ford:** https://en.wikiquote.org/wiki/Talk:Henry_Ford
- Shannon Graham: http://leadersinthetrenches.com/077 (podcast interview)
- **Spencer West:** Climbs Mount Kilimanjaro http://nationalpost.com/news/canada/meet-spencer-west-the-legless-toronto-man-who-climbed-mount-kilimanjaro
- **Joshua Seth:** Finding Focus in a Busy World http://amzn.to/2vOT2Xg
- **Todd Herman:** http://leadersinthetrenches.com/199 (podcast interview)
- **Jim Rohn:** https://en.wikipedia.org/wiki/Jim_Rohn

### Chapter 5

- **John F. Kennedy** - Going to the Moon: https://en.wikipedia.org/wiki/We_choose_to_go_to_the_Moon; https://history.nasa.gov/moondec.html; https://www.jfklibrary.org/Asset-Viewer/Archives/JFKWHA-032.aspx; and https://www.space.com/11772-president-kennedy-historic-speech-moon-space.html
- **Albert Einstein:** https://en.wikipedia.org/wiki/Albert_Einstein; and http://www.quotationspage.com/quote/26032.html
- **Walt Disney:** https://en.wikipedia.org/wiki/Walt_Disney
- **Linda Finkle:** http://incedogroup.com/

- **Stefanie Diaz:** http://leadersinthetrenches.com/245 (podcast interview)
- **Derek Hart:** http://getthegigs.com

## Chapter 6
- **Robin Sharma:** http://www.robinsharma.com/
- **Newfield Network:** https://newfieldnetwork.com/about/

## Chapter 7
- **David Neagle:** http://leadersinthetrenches.com/093 (podcast interview)
- **Seth Godin:** http://www.sethgodin.com/sg/

## Chapter 8
- **Yoda:** http://www.yodaquotes.net/fear-is-the-path-to-the-dark-side-fear-leads-to-anger-anger-leads-to-hate-hate-leads-to-suffering/
- **Mark Twain:** https://www.brainyquote.com/quotes/quotes/m/marktwain141714.html
- **Michael Bungay Stanier:** http://leadersinthetrenches.com/270 (podcast interview); The Coaching Habit: Say Less, Ask More & Change the Way You Lead Forever http://amzn.to/2waBlgo
- **Pat Flynn:** http://leadersinthetrenches.com/134 (podcast interview)

## Chapter 9
- **Mark Zuckerberg:** http://www.businessinsider.com/mark-zuckerberg-is-the-face-of-silicon-valley-2016-4
- **Jason Swenk:** http://leadersinthetrenches.com/006 (podcast interview)and http://leadersinthetrenches.com/130 (podcast interview)
- **Srinivas Rao:** http://leadersinthetrenches.com/222 (podcast interview); Unmistakable: Why Only Is Better Than Best http://amzn.to/2wL1qEA

## Chapter 10
- **Larry Winget:** http://leadersintrenches.com/022 (podcast interview)

## RESOURCES

- **Ron Dod:** http://leadersinthetrenches.com/207 (podcast interview)
- **Warren Buffett:** https://en.wikiquote.org/wiki/Warren_Buffett and https://www.outlookbusiness.com/specials/the-name-is-buffett-warren-buffett/a-successful-investor-knows-when-to-be-arrogant-and-when-to-be-humble-1490
- **Gary Vaynerchuk:** Depth vs. Width https://www.garyvaynerchuk.com/depth-vs-width/
- **Ivan Joseph:** TEDx talk https://ed.ted.com/on/Ji0XuvRh

### Chapter 11
- **Elvis Presley:** https://en.wikipedia.org/wiki/A_Little_Less_Conversation
- **EO Wilson:** https://en.wikiquote.org/wiki/E._O._Wilson
- **Smart Phones:** http://fortune.com/2015/06/29/sleep-banks-smartphones/
- **Informate Mobile Intelligence:** http://www.wsj.com/articles/were-working-more-hoursand-watching-more-tv-1435187603 and http://www.digitaltrends.com/mobile/informate-report-social-media-smartphone-use/
- **Greg McKeown:** http://leadersinthetrenchs.com/211 (podcast interview); Essentialism: The Disciplined Pursuit of Less http://amzn.to/2wLsCTS
- **Jay Papasan:** http://leadersinthetrenches.com/231 (podcast interview); The One Thing: The Surprisingly Simple Truth Behind Extraordinary Results http://amzn.to/2xd8OM8
- **Dale Carnegie:** https://en.wikiquote.org/wiki/Talk:Dale_Carnegie

### Chapter 12
- **Tony Robbins:** Feeding America http://www.feedingamerica.org/hunger-in-america/news-and-updates/press-room/press-releases/tony-robbins-provides-Millions-Meals.html; and I'm Not Your Guru https://www.tonyrobbins.com/documentary/
- **Michael Jordan:** https://en.wikipedia.org/wiki/Michael_Jordan
- **J. K. Rowling:** https://en.wikipedia.org/wiki/J._K._Rowling
- **Brene Brown:** Rising Strong http://amzn.to/2vN0huJ
- **Charles Feltman:** Insight Coaching https://insightcoaching.com/